The Nudge
Writing Prompts

Shana Thornton

Thorncraft Publishing
Clarksville, Tennessee

Cover Design by Shana Thornton

ISBN-13: 978-1-961609-00-6
ISBN-10: 1-961609-00-2

Library of Congress Control Number: 2023939302

Thorncraft Publishing
Clarksville, TN 37043
https://www.thorncraftpublishing.com

10 9 8 7 6 5 4 3 2 1

FOR Rachel, Eddie, and Dani
And all students who ask for writing prompts

Contents

Thematic Prompts 1-110   10

Theme/Vocabulary   53
Prompts 111-162

Historically-Based   76
Prompts 163-180

Creative Writing Basics   83
Prompts 181 -186

Revision Prompts   86
187-190

Self-Reflection Prompts   89
191-203

The Nudge:
Writing Prompts

Introduction

Grab a blank notebook, a manuscript already in progress, or open a new note in your phone. In The Nudge, I give you the writing elbow— a nudge to write on...

In the pages of this book, you will discover writing prompts in a variety of styles. Some of these will speak to you more than others at different times in your life. I encourage you to revisit them again and again. I created these prompts in my own writing journal, and I've returned to it almost daily over the years, whether I need a new approach to a story, to stretch my vocabulary muscles, or to play with words and ideas.

The Nudge began as a weekly writing prompt series in 2017. That first year, I wrote weekly prompts based on different themes and released those on our website and social media platforms for Thorncraft Publishing. Many of the writing prompts also include tools for revision and editing as well as suggestions for reading works of literature reflective of the themes.

There's a prompt series in which I provide inspiration based on a work of art, a fellow writer, or a piece of music. Historically-based writing prompts might inspire new works for you or create a new layer for an existing work.

I've had so much fun sharing techniques and inspiration through this ongoing series. I hope that you enjoy it and that it inspires you to think in new and creative ways about your writing.

The Nudge writing prompts work for the lone writer AND in class settings, writing groups, and between pairs of friends. Good luck and enjoy the writing!

Writing Prompts
1 - 110

#1

DISCOVERY

Open a story by describing a new setting for your character. This is a scene of discovery for your character. They've never experienced this place until now. What are the sensations that accompany this new space? Is this a time of transition for your character, and so can this place represent a transitional space and time?

Additional advice: For nonfiction prose and poetry, consider a place that was unfamiliar to you and describe that transformation— some examples: a new job, a home, moving to a different city, a new room, a park you wandered into, the first time you saw the ocean or mountains.

#2

VALUE OBJECT

What is something deeply valuable to your character? Maybe it is important throughout the character's life. Describe it. Choose a specific time in the character's life to first introduce this object, idea, story, and/or dream to the reader, but consider the full passage of time for the character.

Additional advice: For nonfiction prose and poetry: Is there an object, idea, story, and/or dream that has recurring meaning throughout your life, something you can trace back into childhood and that might have changed in meaning for you over time as well. Tell us a story about it.

#3

CONFLICT EXPLORATION

Free-write and explore the central conflict for your main character. What does your main character most fear regarding the central conflict? What situations cause discomfort for the character and either foreshadow the scenes of central conflict and/or trigger the character (their actions, emotions, motives, etc.) in later scenes.

Additional advice for nonfiction prose and poetry: Write about a conflict that you knew was looming in your life based on foreboding events that preceded the conflict. How does this conflict continue to impact your life, especially in unpredictable ways?

#4
FOOD'S ROLE

Food is essential to life so consider how to incorporate food into your story. Food can be central to the conflict of your story, or it could simply play a minor role in the conflict while still delivering a thematic impact. What role will food(s) play in your story? Free-write about how your character feels about food or the foods that she likes to eat.

Additional advice for nonfiction prose and poetry: Consider a specific food to discuss in your life and/or the overall role of food in your considerations of economics, preservation, and/or sustainability, etc?

#5
NERVOUS HABIT

Create a nervous habit for one of your characters. If not the main character, choose a minor character who needs more description in order to come alive in the story. This habit could add an element of humor and/or realism to your story. The habit could be a sound they make, an action toward themselves or others, or an inability to act. The habit could create a central conflict for the character (consider habits such as cutting, binge eating, and other forms of serious, repetitive self-harming). Likewise, the habit could be more of a side-note, something endearing and entertaining without being central to the conflict. Adding a habit could show more depth to a character or to the overall story.

Additional advice for nonfiction prose and poetry: Most of us have habits that we form as children and can spend a lifetime trying to break, but we also develop new habits as we age. Focus on your own personal habits. Journal until you express more about one of your particular habits than others. How did the opinions/reactions of others influence your habits as you were growing up? Are there habits that you hide and protect, keeping them a secret from the rest of the world?

#6
ENRICHED SETTING

Enrich your story's setting by adding details about the sights, sounds, smells, tastes, textures, and languages found in the story's scenes beyond those expressed by your main character. Consider how much your main character might observe about the setting and/or elements in particular scenes without having a direct experience with those sights, sounds, smells, tastes, textures, and so on. You might want your character to focus on another character at least for a particular scene. Often, this observational stance of the main character can show a comparison/contrast between the main character and a minor character or someone simply passing through the scene of a book. These scenes could reveal how a main character views the setting as a whole or some particular element in the scene, such as a smell, taste, sound, etc.

For example, perhaps your character is sensitive to the sound of someone slurping coffee, and you could show this in a scene by using a stranger at a restaurant or a lunch date with a friend, etc.

Additional advice for nonfiction prose and poetry: Choose a setting and a sense (taste, touch, smell, sight, sound) and fully write about each sense in that setting. How does your writing change if you focus on smell versus sight and so on? How does the sensory experience blend together in some settings/places more than others?

#7
DIALOGUE to SHOW vs. TELL

Read through your story and find a scene in which your narrator tells the reader what happens instead of showing the reader. Often, we get comfortable with a narrative voice in a story and don't allow the characters to show their conversations. One way to accomplish this revision is to use dialogue in a scene where two characters interact, as this allows the characters to speak for themselves versus using a narrator's prose to describe/explain a scene to the reader.

Additional advice for nonfiction prose and poetry: Experiment with how you could use dialogue for emphasis. Consider writing in a specific, unique voice for an entire poem, or suddenly giving a voice to an inanimate object.

#8
RESEARCH

Consider adding another layer to your story by adding actual historical information, data, political events, cultural events and trends, and/or architectural structures to specific settings in your story and/or the plot/events of the story as related to time period in history when the story takes place (or via flashbacks). If your story's time in history is current or futuristic, you could still include references to actual places and work in that information or create new places as if they have been established (in a futuristic work...think about the novel, *Nineteen Eighty-Four*, and how Orwell pulls this off). When you add any of the above styles, it's important not to sound like a textbook or tour guide-style of book, so try to share this type of information in a creative way through a character's experience(s).

Additional advice for nonfiction prose and poetry: Explore a cultural practice that has changed over time and/or through the generations. Write about the shifting perspective of a cultural practice that's related to history and/or tradition.

#9
SMELL

Explore the sense of smell for one of your characters. Free-write about the variety of smells and your characters' reactions. Take this beyond the typical, and consider how a character's sense of smell changes with the different seasons and how the seasons themselves have a variety of fragrances.

What fragrances are pleasant to your character? Do certain scents cause the character to remember his/her past? Are some odors harmful or painful to your characters? Can you add humor to your story or scene by using smell?

Consider how some fragrances change in meaning over time, and how cultures categorize scents in different ways. Also, notice how some people and animals are more keen observers of scent.

Additional advice for nonfiction prose and poetry: Explore one smell for a poem and try to capture the essence of that fragrance. If you have an additional poetic theme, consider writing a series of poems combining your existing theme with the concept of smell. For creative nonfiction, explore how the sense of smell can trigger memories and/or foretell reactions/events to come in the future.

#10
FRAMING MOTIVE
Don't simply consider your narrator's motive for telling the story (or the main character's focus in a third person narrative), think about why they *need to tell the story and how they would frame it. Everyone frames their story just as they dress themselves in clothes, wear a uniform, and alter their appearance in some way. Framing stories is what we do when we tell them, but you get to construct this frame. Does it have flare? Is it simple and straightforward? How will you choose to present your story and why, oh why, is your narrator telling it in the first place? Somewhere in the beginning, you must give the reader a clue about that without giving away the entire story. The reader wants to feel driven to "know it all," so they need a hint about your motive, even if your narrator surprises them later.

Additional advice for nonfiction prose & poetry: Consider juxtaposing one story about your life with another time in your life and link the two by theme or symbol. For poetry, consider "The Rime of the Ancient Mariner" by Samuel Taylor Coleridge as a way of framing a long, narrative poem. The mariner has a need to tell his story.

#11
ROUTINE

Give your character a mundane task or chore that they must repeat and one that you describe in the story. Make this routine, mundane chore suddenly be a moment or event of significant change and/or awareness for your character. Create a surprising twist on the character's approach to this mundane routine and one that resonates through many more aspects of the character's life.

Additional advice for nonfiction prose and poetry: Have you been surprised during a routine occupation such as folding laundry, making coffee, serving someone at a restaurant job, walking to the store on your usual route at the usual time, and/or standing in line at the post office or the bank. Write about an extraordinary moment and/or awareness that happened during a routine.

#12
BASIC MOBILITY
How do your characters stand? How do they walk? Are they incapable of walking/running/jumping for some reason? What does their stride look like if they run? Do they have a particular stance and is it altered when they are nervous or lack confidence? What kind of shoes do they wear? Experiment with basic mobility in your story.

Additional advice for nonfiction prose and poetry: Consider writing about your feet and/or shoes. Do you have a preference for bare feet or keeping your feet covered for some reason? Do you remove your shoes when entering someone's home? Is this related to a cultural stigma or reasons of cleanliness?

#13
SENSE OF STYLE
Let's look at your character's style. Consider how your characters would dress, groom, and otherwise present their physical body to the world. Is your main character superficial in some ways? How? Does your character make a statement or try to shock other people with their appearance, or is your character more concerned with fitting in? Are your character's choices about appearance motivated by cultural demands or restrictions? Are they using appearance to be rebellious and/or political? Does your character care about social, humanitarian, and economic issues regarding industries related to physical appearance?

Additional advice for nonfiction prose and poetry: Consider writing about appearance by focusing on the social impact of trends in an essay or a poem. Think about a specific trend and how that could define people who participate in that trend. On a global scale, write about demands on peoples' appearances based on cultural standards and traditions.

#14
LETTERS

Experiment with the epistolary form in your story. Create a situation in which your character must send and/or receive a letter. Try out the old-fashioned form of snail mail, and/or use more modern methods of sending letters/communications (emails, texts, social media posts and responses).

Additional advice for nonfiction prose and poetry: Consider how your written communications have changed over time. Can you discuss/show how your way of writing to someone has changed, as well as the medium you use to deliver your communications (pen and paper, envelopes, cards, texts, emails, social media posts and responses)? Do you have any letters from the past that you could borrow from in order to create a unique expression of your written correspondences?

#15
MAGIC

Bring in an unexpected moment of magic into your story. Perhaps this magical moment is created by the character being in a special place and/or someone they meet imbues the story with mysticism, mystery, or an otherwise magical presence. Allow this situation to be enchanting and, in some ways, mysterious. The character's life may "go back to normal" afterwards, or the magic could inspire a change in the character or their way of life.

If your character or narrator is on the cynical side, this moment of magic creates something unexpected for the character and the reader. It could reinforce the cynicism in the end, or it could create a contrast that reveals more about the characters.

Magic doesn't have to refer to "hocus pocus." You could use magical realism as a style in part of your story. This means giving magical and/or spiritual qualities or powers to ordinary descriptions and details. Try this approach to your creative nonfiction and/or poetry, if you are not writing fiction. This could also be a time to experiment with blending different genres.

#16
COLOR

Find a scene in your story that needs a little more attention. Revise by focusing on color in that scene. You could emphasize tones of one specific color and relate that to the mood of the scene and/or the overall story. Consider a larger emphasis on subtle details using color throughout your manuscript (clothing, hair color, objects in the environment). Overall, how does your character use or feel about color(s) in his/her life? Do your characters prefer earth tones or bright spaces?

Consider photographs in your story. Could you use black and white or faded photographs in the story to add details and to tell additional stories and histories within your manuscript?

Additional advice for nonfiction prose and poetry: Consider keeping the language and structure simple with a piece like "The Red Wheelbarrow" by William Carlos Williams, while emphasizing the use of color. Or, write about the cultural implications of color and consider a poem like Robert Frost's "The Vanishing Red".

#17
RITE OF PASSAGE

Does your character undergo a rite of passage? How old is your character when she/he first realizes that they will experience a rite of passage? Or, is the experience a surprise or shock? If they know about this experience in advance, is she/he excited, nervous, afraid, etc? Does the character's life truly change after the experience? Does the character feel satisfaction, disappointment, both? Is the rite of passage related to family, culture, religious or spiritual practices, etc?

Additional advice for nonfiction prose and poetry: Explore two different rites of passage in your life— one that you had knowledge of before you experienced it and one that was a shock or surprise to you in some way. If you don't have two experiences, consider comparing one of your own rites of passage to that of someone or something else, perhaps noticing the historical or cultural shifts as one way to approach the theme. For another perspective, consider what it would be like if you were an animal to experience some of the rites of passage that we expect of/ enforce upon animals.

#18
RESEARCH based on PLANT LIFE
Consider the environment/setting where your story takes place. Research the plant life in that environment. Learn about at least one plant that could enrich the symbolism and meaning in your story.

Is the plant classified as a tree, an herb, fruit, vegetable, grass, moss, etc.? How does this plant reflect the state of the environment? Can you relate that to your characters directly or symbolically? Another approach could be to practice blending the characteristics of the plant and its seasonal changes with your character's body and her/his seasonal changes.

Additional advice for nonfiction prose and poetry: Research a plant that you could relate to the state of the environment where you live and write an essay based on the research. Explore the qualities of a specific tree in a particular season for a poem.

For journaling, is there a plant that symbolically connects to your family or that you can trace throughout your life? Why do you think that you are connected to this plant? What do you know about it and could you learn more from studying it/reading about it? How is the plant a representation of you and/or your life?

#19
TRANSFORMATIVE ELEMENT
Bring a transformative element into your writing this week...a dip in a salt bath, a healing tonic, a cooling herb, a visit to the midwife...Is there a curative item, place, and/or person for your character? Consider adding a moment of discovery that is related to an item, person, or place that heals or cures your character. The ailment could be physical, social, psychological, spiritual, and/or all of these. Focus on the moment of healing for your character(s).

Additional advice for nonfiction prose and poetry: Explore a time when you were sick with an illness or disease and write about your body's healing and recovery process. Was there anything that was curative for you or that felt that way symbolically in your life?

#20
SPONTANEOUS CELEBRATION

Say, "Cheers!" Create a spontaneous celebration in your story. This could be a party that your character throws or attends, and/or it could be a small celebratory dinner or drink between two characters. Most importantly, it should happen without a plan. This is something that your character experiences as an impromptu event.

Additional advice for nonfiction prose and poetry: Have you created a spontaneous celebration for any reason in your life? How often do you indulge in celebrating the achievements of your life? Consider when you have allowed the current of the moment to carry you into a celebratory mood, and consider if there was a reason to celebrate or if you were simply answering the zest for life that exists. For poetry, write a celebratory poem. Consider celebrating something that isn't ordinarily celebrated in your culture or family.

#21
ALTERNATIVE TRANSPORTATION
Create a situation in which your character must explore or take alternative modes of transportation than what they are accustomed to in their daily routines. You could place them in a foreign country, where they must use public transportation. You could give them a form of transportation that they must learn as a beginner.

How does your character feel about being out of her comfort zone? Does this inspire her, conjure fears, compel her to try more adventurous ways of moving around in life, etc? If she takes the bus, whom does she meet or see on the bus that prompts a change? What new relationships and/or patterns does the alternative transportation create?

Additional advice for nonfiction prose and poetry: Write about an experience when you unexpectedly had to use a form of transportation that you didn't know was available. Maybe your car broke down and you came up with an alternative. Perhaps you had to walk somewhere as the only means of getting there when you expected something else to happen. Consider exploring several different modes of transportation in your life, and how those have changed over time as you have aged and/or your lifestyle needed a different way of traveling.

#22
FREEWRITE about a MINOR CHARACTER

It's time to have some fun, and play around by exploring the personality of a supporting/minor character in detail. Free-write about a character other than the narrator or main characters; consider characters that might only appear in one scene or animals, pets for example, and even toys as characters. There are truly endless possibilities. After free-writing about the character's personality and/or appearance, etc., write a scene from that supporting character's point of view, even if you don't use it in the final draft of the story. Get to know the supporting character in more detail.

Additional advice for nonfiction prose and poetry: Think back to a scene in your life when a stranger stood out to you, not someone you ever spoke to. Write about someone you observed in real life, but create a poetic or fictional life for them. Make it up, everything about this person. You could set their story in motion from the time that you observed them. Be creative and imaginative about what might be possible in this person's life. You could also choose to write about an animal that you observed as well. Try to write from that entity's point of view as an alternative way of exploring the time in your life, as if they were observing you.

#23
FORMALITIES

Allow your character to attend a formal event. This could be a graduation ceremony, a large wedding, an inauguration, a change of command in the armed forces, an induction, a homecoming, a burial, a consecration, a baptismal, a dedication, a ball, etc.

Is the event somber or festive? Could you inject laughter into a usually somber occasion? Could you bring a sense of foreboding to an event that should be joyful? Is your character comfortable at the event? Does your character notice if others are uneasy with the formalities of the occasion? Allow the character to be transformed in some way by attending the event.

Additional advice for nonfiction prose and poetry: How do these formal events reflect the passage of time in your life? Are they truly transformative moments? What changes beyond your daily routine (for example, when you graduated from high school versus the changes after your college graduation)? Have you ever skipped a formal ceremony (either attending one for someone else or participating in one for yourself)? Why did you choose to skip it? Was it fear, protection, detachment, or some other motivating force?

#24
PREDICTIONS

Allow a prediction to be made about your character. This prediction could be from an oracle or it could be something more akin to a family superstition. Maybe the prediction is made before the character is born, while they are an infant, or during a rite of passage later in life. Consider ancient texts and myths that contain this theme, such as Oedipus Rex and the story of Moses.

Additional advice for nonfiction prose and poetry: Has a prediction been made about you or your life? Was the prediction from your family, a stranger, or something else? If you've never had such an experience, have you ever witnessed someone making a prediction about someone else? Were there events that led them to try to foretell the future? Consider writing about how a prediction about someone's life could be constricting, binding, freeing, and/or enchanting, etc.

#25
REFUGE

Create a place of refuge for your character, a place where they feel safe. Does your character seek the comforts of this place on a routine basis? Is the place indoors or outdoors, both? Does your character ever share this place with others, or is this a place they retreat to in solitude? What activities does your character do in her place of refuge, or does she escape from certain events while there? Show how your character changes after being there.

Additional advice for nonfiction prose and poetry: Write about the changes in your place of refuge over time. The place itself may have changed. Consider writing about what sensory stimuli created a place of refuge for you when you were younger, and what gives you that sense of security now. What are the similarities and differences? We all need places that bring out our true selves at a specific moment in time, and they feel sacred to us for allowing us to be ourselves in that moment, in a way that is secure.

#26

CREATIVE INSPIRATION

What is your character's creative inspiration? Does your character have a positive outlet for her creativity, and have you written about that within the narrative? Does your main character quilt, dance, paint, write, draw, knit, garden, or any other form of artistic expression?

Use this creative practice for your character to add details about not only how this affects your character, but also within your prose as well, to describe the creative action itself. For example, if it's dance that your character uses as a method of self-expression, a job, or a hobby, you can explore and describe elements of dance. Also, consider artistry that's atypical or experimental for your character and story as well.

Additional advice for nonfiction prose and poetry: Choose one of your creative hobbies, not an occupation or job, and write about the reasons why you enjoy this method of artistic expression. Consider the changes you feel during the creative process and after the process is complete for one round or session (for example: a single painting or a dance).

#27

COLLECTIONS

Create a scene in which your character is astounded by a collection. This scene could be only a moment or a longer series of events. The collection could be something your character has acquired over time, or perhaps your character is shown a collection by someone else. Consider typical collections of items such as postage stamps, trading cards, and antiques, as well as unique or odd collections.

Additional advice for nonfiction prose and poetry: Have you ever witnessed or experienced how a collection can become an obsession? Write about how acquiring items can take over someone's life in a way that is unhealthy, versus gathering materials or amassing a collection of something in order to create a grouping to preserve or represent a history or story; for example, a collection of artwork from a specific time period, culture, obscure artist, or region.

#28
RESEARCH COLLOQUIAL CHANGES

All about jive talkin'. Do some research about language and conversation, and include phrases and/or words specific to a certain time period and/or region. Language changes over time and some words are popular only for a short time. Think about how an average word can suddenly have either a positive or negative connotation that changes with the generations. Demonstrate the common parlance of your characters by using dialogue. You might also show changes within a foreign language in your English-written novel.

Additional advice for nonfiction prose and poetry: Focus on one word or phrase and fully explore the colloquial changes in a poem or nonfiction essay. You might also write about the language specific to an industry or occupation and focus on the symbolism of that.

#29
GENEALOGY

Consider family history in relation to your character's motivations and reactions. Show something about your character's family history and explore a family trait, habit, and/or belief. Consider connecting all three in order to fully explore the theme.

Genealogy can be critical if you're writing a book series. Another option is to write out and create a family tree for one or all of your main characters. You can print the family tree in the book(s), or keep it for your own private reference and motivation.

Additional advice for nonfiction prose and poetry: Peruse your own family tree if you have one, or create one based on the information that you have available about your family. Many families record their family trees and histories in family Bibles. One approach to this topic could be to tell a story/write a poem from an ancestor's point of view, based on what little information you might have available to you. You may only know someone's name that strikes you as intriguing and use the name as inspiration to create an imaginary story or one that you try to connect to your own personal story.

#30

PLAYLIST

Writers, get out your toolbox. Time to listen to some music and find your groove with the story. You should have a solid foundation for your story and be familiar with your characters as well as the setting(s) and the time period(s) of the story. Given all of the work you've done so far, stop writing and create a playlist of songs for yourself that's inspired by the story. This isn't necessarily something you will write directly into the story. The music should continue to inspire you while writing your story. The playlist could be composed of songs that you imagine your character(s) would listen to or hear during their time period(s). You might choose to listen to the music while brainstorming or thinking about your story versus while you are actually writing. You could allow the music to inform the mood of your scenes.

Additional advice for nonfiction prose and poetry: Choose a musical genre or a specific artist or song that has influenced your life in some way. Explore the topic of music and its influence in your life. Has your mood changed based on the music in the environment around you? Has music shifted your perspective on something?

#31

RESEARCH a GLOBAL and/or HISTORICAL EVENT

Use an historical and/or global event in your story. This allows you to connect your story with actual events and something that could be in the memory of your readers, especially if you are writing about more modern events. Consider a solar or lunar eclipse as an example of an event many people could experience. Some other examples could be viewing the Northern Lights, warfare that many people experience and/or witness, an earthquake or natural disaster, a meteorite shower, the passage of a visible comet, and more.

Additional advice for nonfiction prose and poetry: Consider writing about an expectation you had regarding a global or historical event that you knew about in advance or that you were certain you would experience, and how the actual experience was different than what you had imagined or expected. For example, if you planned to view the Northern Lights at a particular time, what was that experience actually like? Did it happen? How was it different than you imagined?

#32
"TAKE OUT THE TRASH."

Explore the trash in your story. Write at least one scene that deals with trash in some way. This could be actually taking out the trash or a situation when the character notices the trash somewhere. You might choose to focus on recycling and waste collection. You could write about composting. Regardless, don't fail to acknowledge the trash that exists. Remember, the trash can be both a nuisance and a treasure, depending upon the situation.

Additional advice for nonfiction prose and poetry: Write about how the trash can be a treasure. Consider how people survive based on the trash. You could focus on an occupation that centers on waste removal in some way. Also, think about how the trash has made an impact or been used as a tool. For example, the 1968 AFSCME Memphis Sanitation Workers' Strike during the Civil Rights Movement, or the ways in which trash is used as a weapon or shaming tool during rallies, marches, and boycotts.

#33
MINIMALIST STYLE

Choose a scene or write a new short story and focus on writing it in a minimalist style. You might choose to write in a format and/or with a medium that creates a limitation regarding the length of the work. Consider not simply paring down how many words you use, but perhaps using less characters, punctuation, and/or other common narrative devices. Either way, explore minimalism as a style that sharpens your writing.

Additional advice for creative nonfiction and poetry: Find a tiny, little book to write inside— this will guarantee that your space is limited. You could also use an alternative surface or space that creates a limitation. For examples, consider visual artists who use text as well.

#34
EDUCATION

The focus is on getting schooled. Within a scene or for a chapter or more, write about some aspect of education within your character's life. You could focus on a single teacher, mentor, subject, or class, or you could explore the larger role of education and/or school within your character's life. Consider alternative methods of learning as well as traditional schools.

Additional advice for creative nonfiction and poetry: Write about an education you received that wasn't related to traditional schools or classroom experiences. Maybe this is some form of self-education.

#35
PUBLIC DOMAIN LITERATURE
Find a piece of literature (song, story, poem, book, newspaper article, play) that's now in the public domain. Use a reference to or quotation from that piece of literature. Your character could be influenced by hearing it or reading it. Use this public domain literature simply once in a scene or tie it in to the overall theme of your work, giving it a more significant impact within your piece of writing. Generally speaking, a work becomes part of the public domain about seventy years after the death of the author who owned the copyright. Use this opportunity to do some research and look up the copyright laws for different types of literature and media.

Additional advice for creative nonfiction and poetry: Focus on a piece of literature that influenced your perception about life in some way. The literature impacted you to such an extent that you changed your mind or gained a new perspective completely.

#36
I JUST CAN'T HELP WOOING YOU
Introduce the mood of romance and/or love into your story. Even if your story does not focus on themes of romance and/or romantic and/or passionate love, include a moment, a scene, a memory, and/or a fantasy into the story. Give the reader a little romantic gesture or the full dance. Use this theme of romance to create tension as well. Refrain from going into a full sex scene even if you decide to include one; instead, stay focused on the theme of romance and expressions of romantic/passionate love in this instance, even if you are only hinting at it.

How would your character woo someone? Would she actively pursue a romantic interest? What types of affection and romance arouse your character and get his attention?

Additional advice for creative nonfiction and poetry: Write about a momentary romance in your life. This could be something you only explored in your own imagination— a fantasy that never transpired in real life, or it could be something akin to a "summer romance."

#37
(CRUEL) TWIST OF FATE
It's time to create some empathy in the reader. Add a twist of fate to your story— a turn of events that no one accepts. Consider making this a cruel act of fate or circumstance in life. For example, a character who is waiting for something important and after she moves on and gives up, that something happens without her ever seeing it or knowing it was fulfilled. Shakespeare was clever with using these wicked twists within his plays.

Additional advice for creative nonfiction and poetry: Have you ever wondered how something played out after giving up on it, only to come to the understanding that you will never know? Have you ever become so impatient that you have taken a different route, or given up on a journey due to impatience, and then wondered later what might have happened if you had stuck with the original route or if you had continued the journey? Write about these tricky situations in life, when you wonder if fate is messing with you or prompting you in a certain direction for a reason. Do you think these "alignments of the stars", fate interventions, are real or purely coincidental?

#38
FAIRYTALE ADAPTATION
Find a fairytale or myth and adapt it to contemporary times in a short story or within a section of your story/chapter in your book. There are many examples in films, but consider short stories that achieve this.

Additional advice for creative nonfiction and poetry: Explore a fairytale or myth that you once believed/viewed in a different way than you do now. Create an essay, creative nonfiction story, or poem about how your views concerning this fairytale or myth changed over time.

#39
DREAM SEQUENCE

We've entered the dream time. Add a dream sequence to your story. This dream sequence could be one dream that your character recounts, or you may want to add a more substantial dream scene that brings an element of surrealism to your story. An example of a story that is based almost entirely on the consequences of sleeping/escaping is "Rip Van Winkle" by Washington Irving.

Additional advice for creative nonfiction and poetry: Could you write a nonfiction dream sequence that isn't simply a retelling of a dream? Consider using dreams and dream states in a creative way. Try combining different genres.

#40
WAR

Add an element or awareness of war to your story. Even if war is not part of your overall story at all, you can still create a scene in which your character must think about and consider war as an activity that exists and happens. You could accomplish this by something your character witnesses on television, in the news, by reading a book, or through another character. Often, war can be introduced as a secondary storyline by showing how a relative or a friend of the main character experiences war. The flashback is another technique used to bring in scenes of war to the story and perhaps add an element of surprise at the same time, especially if your readers are unaware of your character's war experience(s) until the flashback scene.

Additional advice for creative nonfiction and poetry: Intertwine your own life with a war experience of someone you know or an ancestor with war experience about which you have heard from other family members. You could blend some historical nonfiction with your creative writing by somehow connecting your lives.

#41
BARBER/BEAUTY SHOP REVELATION

The beauty shop, barber shop, hairdresser, manicurist, etc. have always been popular settings in stories. Often, this setting advances the story and shows a range of characters that represent a time and place. Add a scene to your story in one of these locations. Not only does it allow the reader to see some way that your characters groom and detail their appearance, but the setting allows you to create a revelatory story.

For example, a minor character could tell a confessional-style story during the time at the salon. You could also create a scene of transformation, not only physically but an overall thematic shift could be possible, too. These places give readers a look into cultural practices and trends as well. Consider describing people based on their hairstyles and/or salon preferences.

Additional advice for creative nonfiction and poetry: Think back to your experiences at a barber shop or beauty salon and show how you have changed, not simply your appearance and sense of style, but how you have internally shifted as well. Consider writing about a moment of confession at a salon, whether you were the person who revealed a secret or you overheard someone else telling personal information to their hairdresser and other patrons, etc. You might also think about writing about massage therapy, healing touch, or some other self-care routine similar to a salon experience.

#42
NEW HOLIDAY
Create a scene in which your character experiences a holiday and/or custom that is new to them. This could be a holiday and/or custom outside of their own culture or the culture where they were born, or it could be within their culture and something they've never before experienced. Perhaps you could introduce a new element or theme, some new awareness about the tradition or history of the custom could be another angle to use in your story. If the experience is somewhere other than their home country and culture, allow your character to notice similarities and differences about the traditions.

Additional advice for creative nonfiction and poetry: Write about a time when you learned about the origins of a holiday, tradition, and/or custom and then how that changed either your experience of that holiday and/or your perception of it.

#43
YOU SAY IT'S YOUR (CHARACTER'S) BIRTHDAY?
Write a birthday scene for your character. When is her/his birthday? What have her birthday celebrations been like in the past? Does his

birthday occur on any holidays, major or informal, and/or coincide with anyone else's birthday? Maybe a major life event takes place on her birthday.

Additional advice for creative nonfiction and poetry: Let's write a poem or short nonfiction piece from an alternative perspective while still focusing on the self or nonfiction. Write about your birthday from the perspective of someone else. Consider your birthday vibe from the perspective of your parent, sibling, relative, partner, child, and/or friend. How do you treat others on your special day? Do you have a sense of entitlement concerning your birthday? Perhaps you shut out others on your birthday, forfeiting your chances to celebrate or to spend time with other people in your life, or maybe your birthday lasts for a whole week and is full of merriment and joy for being alive. Try taking a look back from an alternative angle.

#44
ARCHITECTURE
Focus on the architecture within your setting. You may choose to write in detail about one particular building or structure. You could also describe a city or section of a place. Another angle would be to create feelings that your character might have about a certain building or place and/or the architecture of the town where your character lives or is visiting.

Additional advice for creative nonfiction and poetry: Have you been attached to certain architectural structures in your life? Consider any historical buildings or places that hold meaning for you. Have you experienced the destruction of places that were valuable to you or others? Why was the architecture significant? You could also consider how architectural presence creates the mood of a street or section of a town. Have you witnessed a shift in mood when the architecture of a place changes or is altered? Also, as another angle, consider any stories associated with architectural structures, whether those are superstitions, historically documented tales, or other legends and lore associated with architectural structures.

#45
VOICE
We're paying attention to sound and voice. Describe your character's voice in every way. You should consider if your character has a loud

or soft voice, any squeaks or little nervous ticks when he speaks, stuttering or sing-song habits in certain situations, and accents or second languages. Does your character have a plain speaking voice but a beautiful singing voice? Think about the different ways to describe and write about voice in order to make your character's more distinctive. Consider other sounds that your character could make with her voice even when she isn't speaking (for example, when eating, sleeping, driving, exercising, meditating, etc.)

Additional advice for creative nonfiction and poetry: Write about the contrasts of sound and voice. For example, you could focus on the loss or limitation of your voice. Was it temporary or a more permanent situation? How did the loss or limitation of your voice effect how you experienced sound? You could also write about voice amplification. Have you experienced the unnecessary amplification of your voice or someone else's and noticed how that over-expression of sound caused others to feel?

#46
FURNITURE
Is it possible to refine your descriptions of the interior details in your settings? Do you tend to skip over descriptions of furniture and use a singular noun (for example, chair, bed, table, etc.) in every situation? Could you, sometimes, be more specific in your descriptions of furniture and furnishings without going overboard with those details?
The furniture in a story can be used to date the setting or even the time period of the story. Use furniture as a way to trigger a scene of reverie. Your character might be interested in the furniture for sentimental reasons, or he may simply notice some household item while visiting someone.
Use furniture in a subtle way, or in a more pronounced moment to show anger and rage. For example, perhaps your character takes her anger out on a malfunctioning piece of furniture.

Additional advice for creative nonfiction and poetry: Use a piece of furniture or a furnishing to shape an entire poem. Consider ways to emphasize the traits of that furniture. For example: Shel Silverstein's "Furniture Bash". For nonfiction, experiment with imagination. Was there a piece of furniture or a furnishing that held a magical quality for you as a child? While it is fiction, consider C.S.

Lewis' "The Lion, the Witch, and the Wardrobe" from *The Chronicles of Narnia* as an example.

#47
GAMES
People play games in life, so think about the types of games that your character plays. If you're writing an historical novel or story, this gives you an opportunity to add a scene that shows a game that may now be out of fashion. Be creative and have fun with playing games in your story. Example, My own novel, *Poke Sallet Queen and the Family Medicine Wheel,* contains a scene in which secrets are revealed over a card game of Hearts.

Additional advice for creative nonfiction and poetry: Focus on a game that you no longer play but that was important and pivotal in your past. Show your transformation from the time when that game was your focus and why you became enamored with it in the first place, to how you lost interest or moved away from it, as well as how it shaped who you have become now. Consider showing how easily a game can lead to an obsession of some sort, whether that is winning or some other scenario.

#48
SEASONS OF NATURE
If you tend to avoid writing about nature, let's try some subtle revisions on the setting throughout your novel, or choose a particular recurring place in your setting, AND show the changes of the seasons. In this way, you can show the passage of time, and nature can be a more active element in your story. If you tend to lean away from descriptions of nature in your writing, focus on a single natural cycle and symbolize that complete cycle.

Additional advice for creative nonfiction and poetry: Choose an element of nature, other than the human experience, whether you focus on a plant, animal, mineral, or a land formation, and write about that natural element's cycle of life. Even though you may even write from your own point of view, focus on the seasons of life that accompany whatever life form or natural process you choose.

#49
Point of View, ANIMAL'S STORY
Write a scene or short story from an animal's point of view. This could be a wild animal or a domesticated pet. If you're incorporating this story into a longer work or novel, consider using the point of view of your character's pet for an experimental scene or chapter. This is an opportunity to be imaginative and creative. Perhaps the animal is the first person narrator.

Additional advice for creative nonfiction and poetry: Return to a memory from your past that involved an animal. Write about that moment from the animal's perspective. Imagine. Explore. Consider possibilities that you might have overlooked by focusing on yourself or your own point of view.

#50
DUSK
Write about dusk— that transition time from daytime to evening. Consider writing about dusk from a couple of different settings or locations, as well as from different points of view. You might also explore how the feeling of dusk changes in the winter versus how a character experiences dusk in the spring or summer.

#51
APOLOGIES
Perhaps the apology comes in the form of an unexpected letter. Perhaps you use a casual meeting to deliver a long lost, "I'm sorry." Does your character have that nervous habit of apologizing for everything he does? Are they ruthless about forgiveness after an apology? Does your apology scene include a confession, healing, redemption?

If you write nonfiction or poetry, draft one of your own— an apology to yourself, a letter. Write an essay about apologies— how they've played out in your life, what you were taught about them as a child, if you were ever forced into them as a child and/or an adult, and if you require them in your relationships.
And, consider the feelings that show up after an apology.

#52
LEAVING
Write about the act of leaving someone, something, or a place behind, of being left behind, and/or the choices of having to leave a place, a person, a title, a situation, a belief, etc.

Some questions: Was it a sudden decision out of necessity? What led to the act of leaving? What foreshadowed the decision? What secondary people, places, ideas, beliefs, etc., were shed as a consequence of the primary act of leaving? What were the surprises along the way?

#53
TREES
Just a few ideas... Use them in your setting, in your story, as more than ornamentation. Find out about a particular kind of tree and let your story revolve around it. Pick a favorite tree and write an ode to it. Give your character a favorite tree or maybe one that annoys her. Invite a nuisance into your story because of a tree. Write a poem about a tree and allow it to tell the story of that place. Dig deep and learn the particulars. Make a character or a cast of them out of trees. Consider how the life of the tree and the life around the tree changes depending on the season and the weather. Perhaps, if you are able to do so, go outside and write while sitting underneath or near to a tree. And, so on...

#54
MISSED OPPORTUNITIES
Give your character an experience in which they realize that they missed an opportunity, one that they will never get back. Allow them a scene of grief for the awareness of the loss in their lives.

#55
PHOTO BOOTH SCENE
Or, maybe you write a whole story that centers on a photo booth. This photo booth could be an "old style" photo booth of various sorts, or it could a modern photo booth with a computer connected to it that allows you to change backgrounds and records the footage of the photo booth during a wedding reception or some other modern extravaganza. Be creative about where you place your photo booths and what happens inside of them.

#56
VACATION TRAGEDY

Shape a story around a vacation that goes wrong. Allow at least one of the characters to have a premonition at the beginning of the story that something will go wrong. This could be a humorous mishap or a tragic event that leaves the characters devastated.

#57
VOTING

Write a story or scene about the experience of voting and/or not voting, though make the central theme of the story or scene about the process of voting. Some examples: write about a character who volunteers at the polls, someone who registers others to vote, a character who is conflicted about the process of voting, a character who can't vote for some reason, and/or a character's life changes because of their views about politicians, the process of voting, how other people in their life vote, etc.

#58
DINNER TABLE

Center a short story or a whole chapter for a longer work around a single meal at the dinner table. Try not to change locations or settings. Describe the meal itself as if it is a character or a group of characters. Allow it to affect your characters and their actions. Don't simply describe the food based on fragrance and flavors. Go beyond those basic descriptions of food.

#59
MIRRORS

Use a mirror and/or objects that mirror in order to write a scene in a longer work or a complete story that centers on mirrors. Draw inspiration from the stories of Narcissus in Greek mythology, the Snow White fairytale by the Brothers Grimm, and "Through the Looking-Glass" by Lewis Carroll. Create your own modern twist on mirrors/screens and objects that mirror.

#60
GOODBYES

Write a last call, final round, going away, leaving the building, arrivederci, "see ya later, alligator," one more hug, wave bye-bye scene. Try writing a goodbye scene at the beginning of a story, book, or poem. Where does that lead you in the course of the story?

For nonfiction, have you ever felt as if saying goodbye was a relief in your life and allowed you start over?

#61
HARD TO FIND INGREDIENT
Add a rare, hard to find, ingredient to the story. Maybe the ingredient is only a challenge to locate based on where your characters are, or perhaps the conditions of the time have limited something that's usually abundant, or perhaps it's available if only your characters could get to it. This might not be a food ingredient for a dish or a meal, but it might be a symbolic ingredient.

#62
CEMETERIES
Write a scene in a cemetery. This could be a typical burial or visitation scene, but perhaps you think of some other situation that causes your character to end up in a cemetery. Maybe she is passing through on her way to another location, or perhaps she accidentally finds herself at the cemetery while taking a walk. Your character might discover a cemetery somewhere on his property.

For nonfiction, consider the funerals and/or burials you've attended and write about those. Have you observed a funeral or burial for someone you don't know? Contrast your grief/mourning in your experience with the grief/mourning you've witnessed in other people.

#63
SIBLING/FRIEND RIVALRY
Write about a sibling rivalry but with an added twist. The dynamic between the siblings could change when a competitive friend or acquaintance joins them. Do the siblings join forces and take up for one another, or do they escalate their competition and try to force the friend to choose sides?

#64
PARENT COMPETITION
Does your character's parent compete for attention with him? Does his dad try to beat him in every sport and/or game that they play?

Does her mom correct her behavior, words, appearance, etc? Create a competitive atmosphere between your character and their parent(s). How does this affect your character as he ages? Do their relationships change over time?

#65
A WINDOW

Describe the world passing by a window. What sounds can be heard through the window? Are they muffled? Is the window ever open? Describe the fragrances that drift through the window. Perhaps something comes in through the window that is unexpected.

#66
SEED PACKETS

Use the images from heirloom seed packages and advertisements to inspire your writing. Read the descriptions of the plants and growing conditions. Allow these to inform your writing. Consider comparing the heirloom packets and advertising for seeds and plants that you can still find today. Are there any that you can't find?
Examples: In music, The Squirrel Nut Zippers album *Perennial Favorites*. My book covers for *Poke Sallet and the Family Medicine Wheel* and *Ripe for the Pickin'* were inspired by heirloom seed packets.

#67
CHILDREN'S ARTWORK

Look around at some artwork by children and use that in your writing. Maybe something is revealed to your character through his child's artwork from school. Perhaps a child character of yours uses art as an outlet to express her frustration. Examples: You can find the contributions of children to modern art installations and community projects. Many times, Museums offer interactive exhibitions and/or spaces where children create their own artwork in response to what they have viewed and/or learned. If you have children in your life, their artwork might provide the inspiration.

#68
ANCIENT TEXTS

Ancient texts, such as: *I Ching, Tao Te Ching, Yoga Sutras, Upanishads, Book of the Dead, Epic of Gilgamesh,* or some other text with philosophical, ethical, and/or moral ways of life. Try using one philosophical idea from an ancient text within your modern story or poems. One approach is using a quotation at the start of a chapter or section, and then allowing the characters to exemplify the idea expressed in the quotation. Another approach is allowing the character to be interested in a particular philosophy and sharing those ideas through the character.

#69
SENSE OF WONDER

Let's travel, for a moment, to a place in your memory that was dreamy and intoxicating, a time when you felt swept up in a frenzy of momentum and exhilaration. Give that feeling a setting, maybe it doesn't go along with the setting of your memory and that's just fine. Allow yourself to daydream and invent a landscape that gives you a sense of wonder and excitement if you can't think of one from past experience. And then, allow the character you place there to be surprised by the reality of the place. Perhaps it's more challenging to be there than she thought, or maybe he doesn't like the local customs of a new landscape.

#70
GHOST STORY OR LEGEND

Let's use a real legend or scary story as inspiration for one of your own stories or poems. For example, the Wood Booger, the name of the Sasquatch or Bigfoot in Central Appalachia. Allow the Wood Booger to disrupt the life of one of your characters, or perhaps you write something from the perspective of the Bigfoot legend herself. Does the Wood Booger have to be a male? How can you adapt a legend to make it your own? Could you recreate an ancient story and update it? How about making the Wood Booger a character who evokes sympathy from the reader? Example: The Headless Horseman from Washington Irving's "The Legend of Sleepy Hollow"

#71
DANCE

Write a dance scene in your story. This might be a provocative dance scene or something funny to interrupt the narrative. You could use a cast of strangers as the characters in the dance scene, and perhaps you find these strangers within a painting or photograph. For example, write about the scene depicted in "El Jaleo" by John Singer

Sargent. Artwork is a unique and wonderful way to bring imagery from another imagination into your literature and blend the two.

#72
DANCE INVITATIONS

We're practicing how to be versatile writers. If you used the last prompt to find a piece of artwork and write a dance scene based on it, we're going a step farther this prompt and looking into how everyone came to be there. Look back at your dance scene and determine who the main players are in the scene, even if they are characters who were new to the story and who you thought were only going to emerge one time in the story. Identify the main players. Other than your main character, write a rough sketch for how a character came to be there at the dance. What were the circumstances that led these characters to this moment in time with your main character? Get into the background of these characters.

Example: In *A Momentary Darkness* by Nikki Martin, first we see how Kale came to be at the cliff, and then we see how Derrin arrived there in a later scene from his perspective.

#73
OBSESSION

We're looking at character traits, specifically the little quirks that make some characters stand out. Give one of your characters an infatuation with some type of cosmetics or cosmetic procedures. For example, your character might be obsessed with avoiding gray hair, so he dyes his hair every chance he gets and is repeatedly looking in the mirror to see if his hair is turning gray. Maybe you have a character who won't go out of the house in sandals if she doesn't have a pedicure on her feet, or a character who won't purchase certain shampoos depending on the name they are given by the brand. Get creative with consumer culture and give your character an obsession related to it. This could be a minor story in their lives, or one that becomes a major storyline and has great consequences.

#74
MESSAGE IN A BOTTLE

Cue the music by Sting, we're adding the arrival of a mysterious message into our story. This is a message in a bottle type of situation. Someone called out into the world in decades past and their message has resurfaced into your main character's life. Perhaps your character wrote a message or letter long ago and then forgot about it, only to have it or a response show up when she never expected that it would. Does it revive memories for your character? Do people return into his life along with the words from the past? Example: In *The Mosquito Hours* by Melissa Corliss DeLorenzo, Vivian's long-hidden journals are discovered by her daughter.

#75
THE SEARCH

Take your character on a quest for a sacred object. Perhaps you bring the idea into the modern world and the sacred object is something common to the 21st century. You might still endow this object with magical powers or perhaps it bestows a gift on the owner, or some other fairytale storyline within your contemporary novel. Maybe you consider the origins of the object if it is something antique or historical that becomes valuable in contemporary times. Consider breaking the gender roles and norms as you write your quest.

If you're journaling, what do you think about possessions containing special energies or powers? Do you think the circumstances of a thing's creation can shape the energy that it carries? Or, have you witnessed these beliefs as damaging superstitions or tools to pass judgment on the lives of others?

Example: In *A Momentary Darkness* by Nikki Martin, Kale has this same sacred quest challenge, and she is the heroine of the story.

#76
LOVE LETTER

Epistolary stories create the impression of being privy to a personal exchange between two people. Letters within a story give you a chance to practice the confessional, when one character confesses something to another within a letter. You might try love letters, a secret admirer's missives, stolen letters, or the long-lost family member who reaches out after decades. These are only a few examples. Letters allow you to play with dialect and a writing voice or multiple voices. You might even bring the idea of letter writing into contemporary times and use emails and messenger apps as the framework of the story. Tinker with letter writing, and maybe even use the sentiment in a real life letter that you have received to get you started. Examples: In *Grace Among the Leavings*, by Beverly Fisher, the letters now only reveal a secret about Grace's mother, but they also show us the postal system, Grace's reading level, the literacy of her grandparents, and so much more.

#77
HEADLESS STATUE OR FACELESS PAINTING
Statues and artwork have been defaced throughout history. One example is the "Winged Victory of Samothrace" housed in the Louvre. In literature, we find many examples, and one is in the headless horseman of "The Legend of Sleepy Hollow" by Washington Irving. In my own novel, I write a scene of sculptural and cultural defacement in *Multiple Exposure*. In children's literature, Lewis Carroll evokes the sentiment through the Queen of Hearts, as she demands, "Off with their heads!" in *Alice's Adventures in Wonderland*.

Can you think of some way to add this idea to your writing? Does your character encounter a faceless work of art that otherwise depicts the human form? What does this "headlessness" or "faceless" state reflect about a culture, both the one that created it and the one responsible for its defacement?

#78
THE TOPIARY
That's right, the garden bushes that might be shaped like a rabbit or boxed neatly, trapping you in a labyrinth. Think of the haunted hotel, but the topiary hedges offered their own terrors. Perhaps they don't have to be so frightening, but dark comedy also comes to mind. How does the topiary trip unfold? Your character might undergo a tussle under the boxwoods? A rolling of heads among the roses, as in Lewis Carroll, croquet? What about you, dear writer, what shall you do with the topiary scene? ...Or, maybe you say "a trip through topiaries" a few times and write some tongue twisters.

#79
THE DARE
Maybe it's a game of truth or dare, or perhaps it's more subtle than that and the dare isn't vocalized but is understood based on past

actions and attitudes. A dare doesn't have to be negative. Consider ways in which a dare can be turned around to the advantage of the character.

I dare you to give your characters some challenges in the form of a dare from someone else. Try both the direct, spoken dare as well as the implied dare.

#80
VISIT FROM A HISTORICAL GHOST
Bring in several historical people whose paths cross with the characters in your novel. Some of these historical people aren't famous or well-known when they interact with your characters. Are these family legends and/or tall tales? Does your family have any stories about famous or well known people? Use those ideas in your fiction.

#81
A CROWD
Consider writing about not a random crowd but a crowd with a purpose. The crowd could be an organized protest, an unorganized riot, perhaps a movement with a goal. Does your character witness it or is she a part of it? Maybe she sees it from afar, or he could be suddenly immersed in the crowd without planning to be a part of it. Your crowd might also originate due to a concert or a large sporting event.

#82
A PHILOSOPHY
Perhaps this way of life changes your character and her experiences. Some examples from history are the Surrealist Manifesto or the zeitgeist movement. A current philosophy along with an example of a current writer you can search out is pronoia, the belief that life is positive and offering to bless you and known as the opposite of paranoia. Have fun with diving into philosophy as you write, and allow your character to have some fun with it, too.

#83

END OF LIFE CELEBRATION

Write an end of life celebration scene. Consider what the speaker, minister, or spiritual guide says to the mourners. Is there a eulogy? Maybe you add an obituary to the scene. What special rituals are performed? Do they coincide with the dead's wishes? You might write two scenes, one inside a building such as a funeral home and/or one outside at a burial site or location to spread the ashes of the deceased.

For nonfiction: Consider writing your own obituary as a way of practice your writing and self-reflection. Examples: In *Talking Underwater* by Melissa Corliss DeLorenzo, we witness the anger and anguish between the two sisters at the dinner after the funeral.

#84

BODY DETAILS

Go through your manuscript and look at where you added details about your characters' physical body. Could you be even more specific? Can you go beyond the basic descriptions of the body— hair color, height, weight, etc.— and write about more of your character's body. Their knuckles and fingertips, their cuticles and fingernails, all have details. Could you focus on the feet? The soles of a character's feet— are they blistered, sore, bruised, scarred? Or maybe your character's face reflects a particular way of listening, a way of looking out over a landscape, a way she changes when she is driving, a flare he adds to his hairstyle when he goes to a particular place. Does your character have wrinkles across his forehead when he answers the phone, or perhaps she always arrives at the coffee shop and picks the sleepy matter from her eyes while ordering her first cup of coffee for the day? Have some fun while writing the details of your character's physical body.

#85

PACING

Let's look at pacing this week. Think in terms of walking or running. If you consider a movie, when the characters run, the action of the story picks up. If a character is walking who needs to run, the tension increases in the film. The same can be true for your writing style. When you write in sentence fragments or short, choppy sentences, you add speed to the manuscript's flow. Sentence fragments can signal distress, confusion, or excitement. When you use a character who takes a very long time to explain something important, then you add tension to the story. A character who speaks in commands might add even more tension.

Or, you could write in long, flowing sentences to allow the reader to linger in the setting. Sentence structure and dialogue structure can further add to the pacing that you want to create for the story and ultimately for the reader. The pacing often determines how quickly the reader can read your work. Complex sentences require a more careful reading of the story.

On your mark, get set, and alternate the pacing of your story depending on what you want to accomplish.

#86
A PICNIC SCENE
Create a picnic scene this week. Find a work of art, perhaps something from a top 10 list of picnic paintings if you search online, as visual inspiration.

You might also take yourself on a picnic and use the experience to set up a scene in your book.

In your story, is the picnic planned or spontaneous? What food and drinks does your character bring along, or does she need to find food and decide to have a picnic somewhere she's never explored? What do the characters discover around themselves during the picnic? What does your character reveal about himself from that moment of slowing down and enjoying a meal outside? Picnics can be revealing and intimate, so allow moments to show vulnerability and observation. Examples in literature: *Talking Underwater* by Melissa Corliss DeLorenzo includes picnics at the beach, and a comparison of those times when Amy was a child to when Amy is an adult.

#87
A BRIDGE SCENE

Write a bridge scene or an actual bridge (for a song). Writing music? Practice writing a bridge to your most recent song. This is your chance to play on the harmony and give the song a little extra moment.

Writing a scene in a novel or short story? Add a bridge to the setting. There are famous bridges where you might place your character(s). You might also choose some less famous ones. The many wooden bridges in national and state parks come to mind. Toll bridges are another type of bridges that are frequently crossed. How can you use a bridge as a symbol in your story? How can the bridge act as a tool for you, as a writer, a method of how you move the story as well?
The bridge could also serve as the opening or the closing of your book or poem.

Don't forget to consider perspective when writing the scene. Consider writing the bridge scene from both a high and a low perspective, as well as from each side, if you want to practice point of view in the sense of physical placement. You might be surprised by where it leads and how it changes the story when written from other perspectives.

#88
FIRE

Practice using fire in your writings. First, free-write about fire, and free associate your ideas about fire with other topics and see what comes out of it. Take no more than fifteen minutes to free-write and free associate. Use the strongest and most unique images and ideas to craft a poem and/or a short story using fire as a main theme, symbol, or element in the writing.

In a novel, you might use the idea of fire. How can you use fire without being literal?

#89
SAND

Let's use sand as a part of the story. You might use sand as a symbol and only refer to verbs and descriptions that conjure the idea of sand without using it literally. Then, there's the sand; write about the texture of it, the changes it undergoes as it is wet and becomes dry, the warmth or coolness of the sand against skin. You might consider writing about the different landscapes of earth that are dominated by sand. In these places, some of the sand is a shoreline, bordering water, holding pines, and becoming the bane of tourists who get to leave it behind; in other places, the sand carries on for miles and vast stretches in every direction, piling up hillsides and dunes, that topple over themselves as if they will never end; the sand of mountaintops and plateaus surprises people; the land on lakes and riverbanks shakes out into rocks and stones. Enjoy this moment of writing with the sand, and consider allowing the land to be a medium, as it is in sand paintings, the way that a shaman created them, read the meanings and transformations, and the elements wiped the images and the messages away.

You could also have your character walk out into the sand, take off his shoes, and step into another life. What would it be?

#90
WATER
The element of water represents vitality and life on the planet. Allow your character to experience water in a new way, noticing the subtle shifts in water's ability to soothe and calm as well as to cause discomfort and/or tragedy. Consider the ways that water is mesmerizing and transformative, the ways in which people and life in general adapt to the shifts in the water in an environment. The water is magnetic— to people, to electrical energy, to animals and creatures, to plants, as well as to fragrance. Maybe you consider how water collects and filters.

You might also choose an environmental slant to your writing this week. Discuss the availability of clean water sources on the planet. Free-write about times when you have taken the water for granted or explore the feeling of having limited water to drink and use or none at all. You might consider writing a contrast essay about water usage in the past to modern day water usages.

Some examples of great writing about water and watery environments can be found in Melissa Corliss DeLorenzo's *Talking Underwater*, Melissa dives into the love and the fear of water.

#91
THE MOUNTAIN

You could discuss the ways that the dirt and rock on a mountain shift and change, creating a moving landscape where there is the idea of stability. The Mountain is symbolic of strength. Maybe you use this typical symbolism of the mountain in your story. Also, consider writing about the vulnerability of the mountain, places where it is fragile. Or, write about the life on the mountain that is fragile. You might also write about the extreme highs and lows discovered on the mountain. The height of the peak in the sky and clouds. The depths of the ravines in the dark and watery places. Use those changing views to symbolize more about your characters— one place on the mountain might provide a lookout over an expansive vista, where she feels freedom, while another location on the mountain blocks the character's view. She might feel protected, or she might feel trapped by this limitation on the mountain. You might also approach this topic by using humor. Write about a time when you were on a mountain, and it was not what you expected it to be.

Check out paintings by Zen Buddhists that feature mountain landscapes. These images can be helpful when writing in a minimalist style.

#92
METAL

Have you thought about allowing metal to be the star of your setting? Have you ever focused on the metals of a cityscape or those found in a landscape? Sometimes, metal surprises you, jutting up from the forest, a remnant of the past, a time when a place was used differently: Pipes in a cave, old fences, an abandoned car, a piece of farm equipment covered with layers. There's metal as it connects to the human body--the taste of metal, body parts made of metal, metal as assistance, adornment, and/or protection.

#93
SUN AND MOON

Maybe the sun and the moon seem as if they'd be obvious choices to inspire creative writing. They are so often used in descriptive passages, moments of contemplation for the characters. How can you make them a featured character for more than simply a passing description of their effects on the landscapes? Push sun and/or moon into a greater expression. Think of some obvious examples, Ancient Greek tales of gods and goddesses, who are often intertwined with celestial bodies, seasons of the year, and a combination of elements, both human and other. What about your writing? Could you incorporate these techniques, with the sun and moon as inspiration?

#94
STONE/ROCK

Use stones or rocks in your writing in order to show opposing positions, to symbolize paradox, to give mixed messages. Stones move and make sounds, though we think of them as silent and immovable. We need rocks and pebbles, though they can be a pain as well. You might choose to write about stone that is molded into vessels, tools, and weapons by people, or the stones (fossils) that have been shaped into patterns by water and wind. Write about large stones, mountains, that have captivated people for different reasons. Mt. Rushmore is an example. You might consider writing about places that are sacred as it relates to the formation of the earth (the way that stones and rocks stack up and look, or the spaces that are created with stones by people). An example is the famous Stonehenge in Wiltshire, England.

#95
A CHILD'S QUESTION

The child's question allows you to explore many different directions in a narrative. A question from a child can cause adults to see a new perspective, especially since children seem to ask questions "out of the blue." A child's question could lead unknowingly to an internal dilemma for the adult or some type of existential crisis. The question might prompt an investigation to find out the answer, leading to an unexpected and fun experience, maybe even a quest. Toddlers can sometimes ask questions until adults become aggravated or even angry, so adding questions to your narrative could create a simple way to display and make way for emotions that then allow you to delve into other parts of the characters' psyches. The responses to a child's questions can be fun, entertaining, baffling, confusing, disturbing, dismissive, and so much more. Try different responses to the same question as a way of practicing your craft of characterization.

#96
WIND

Maybe you think of clichés right away--the winds of change, no wind in the sails, the sacred *all* of the wind--immortalized in song and hymn, in jokes, in anecdotes by relatives, in constant discussions of the weather and Chicago, the plains, dustbowls, the lands of Oz revealed during tornadoes.

Clichés, aside, what can you do as a writer with the wind? How has it shaped you, influenced your sense of smell, piqued your awareness by rustling the whiskers of your character's grandmother's chin, wafted the pollen across the horizons of your stories in an afternoon glowing above cricket songs?

#97
GRASS

Write about different types of grass, how they feel on your feet, the ways that people try to get rid of grass, the complaints about having it as well as not having it, and the variety of ways that people care for it, from mowing it to watering it. Think about how views of grass have changed with time.

You might approach this topic by writing about the insects, arachnids, other plant life, and more that lives in and is affected by grass.

#98
PUZZLES

Layer a story so that it represents a puzzle, and perhaps you have a puzzle show up in the story somewhere. This could be a cardboard cut-out puzzle that a character puts together, but it might be a crossword puzzle or some other type of mental puzzle.

Maybe you get very creative and write your paper out onto paper or cardboard and create some type of puzzle of your own.

#99
STRETCHING
Write about a moment of stretching and make something odd happen during this pause. Maybe a character gets up to stretch her legs and take a walk after sitting at a desk all day. Perhaps she stretches her arms overhead and hits something. Maybe the stretch is a yawn from a character. Or, go for the sports scene and write about stretching for an event or competition.

#100
SOUNDS IN THE DISTANCE
Perhaps your character hears an unfamiliar sound in the distance and follows it. Maybe it's a repetitious sound. It might lead to an unexpected adventure. Your character could also hear singing in the distance. Maybe curiosity compels her to track down the singer over time. You could use this as opportunity to create a disappointment, something that the character creates in her mind based on a sound she hears, but the reality is a letdown, and maybe her imagination was so much more interesting than what she discovers as the source. The sound could also be coming from nearby. Think of Edgar Allan Poe's "The Tell-Tale Heart."

#101
PREY DEFEATS PREDATOR
Create a scene or story in which the prey outwits and/or defeats a predator. If you can create an element of surprise for the reader at the same time, that would be great.
In my book, *The Adventures to Pawnassus*, Mia's mom sees a wild turkey mom kill a snake that was going to harm her baby turkeys.

#102
GLASS
Allow the inspiration of glass into your story. Notice how glass reflects and illumines. You might also describe the sounds of glass, superstitions surrounding, how it is made, and the allure of glass. Consider how we are fooled by glass and how it reveals.

#103
NEGOTIATIONS

Create a scene of suspense and negotiations. Don't make this an easy negotiation for the reader or for the characters. Keep everyone guessing. Perhaps you set it up in the scenes leading up to the final negotiation so that you can pull the rug out from beneath the reader and the characters.

#104
FAILED GARDEN
Describe a failed garden for your character. This could be a simple container garden or it might be something more devastating such as a failed crop on the family farm business. Maybe a blight and/or drought affect the plants. You could contrast a once healthy garden with one that has been devastated in some way, or you might show that the garden never grew at all in the first place.

#105
TO-DO LIST
Give your character a to-do list and use it to write a story or poem.

#106
GROCERY LIST
Give your character a grocery list and use it to write a story or poem.

#107
TOILETS
It's time for your character's bathroom break. Maybe they encounter a particularly clean and refreshing bathroom, or perhaps they must use a bathroom that traumatizes them. There are a variety of toilets in the world, so take some time to write about at least one of them as a practice session.

#108
BEDS
Write about a bed. Maybe you describe a variety of them for a variety of species. Or, focus on one bed for one character. Write a love scene, dream scene, relaxing scene, funny moment, scary situation, all of the above.

#109
TEXTS

Write a text exchange in your story. Make these important text messages in your story. They should influence in the story. Don't include boring and plain text message passages that don't add anything to the overall story.

#110
HOPE

Write about a hope that your character has for the future. Maybe you don't include this in the actual story, but it shows you, the writer, what secretly motivates your character. Often, people don't share their hopes with other people but those hopes are harbored in their minds and imaginations and keep them focused on their goals in some way. Explore this idea for your characters.

For nonfiction and poetry: Write about how your ideas about hope have changed as you've gotten older. Do you have the same views but express them more now? Did you express them more as a child or youth than you do now? Do you think hope is a sentimental idea or do you think it is crucial for positivity and/or success?

Themes and Vocabulary Words
Prompts 111 - 162

New prompt style for The Nudge. I will provide a theme and a group of words. These words could be nouns, adjectives, adverbs, and/or verbs. You may choose to approach this writing prompt style in a variety of ways. You could use this as a challenge to add words to your story or manuscript that you may not otherwise have used. Another option is for you to learn the definitions of the words, if you don't know them already, and practice usage of the words in order to incorporate them into your vocabulary. You may also approach these prompts by learning word etymology, delving deeper into the meaning of the word throughout history, and bringing that knowledge into your writing. Be creative as you learn and use words from these prompts. Challenge yourself to use all of the words in a single poem or short prose piece, or even to use them in conversation during the day. Take note of which words are easy and which are difficult or awkward to incorporate into your spoken vocabulary or your particular style of writing.

#111
BLENDING
Write about blending. Maybe this is blending drinks, something obvious, or perhaps it's about blending wildlife into nonnative areas.

VOCABULARY WORDS:
accoutering
dawn
listless
malleable

#112
LATE NIGHT DRINK
It's time for some late night word play in the style of Hemingway and Fitzgerald and all of their friends. Grab a drink, settle in, and conjure up something akin to an evening wandering around Paris. See what you can make out of this week's word list. Cheers!

VOCABULARY WORDS:
distractible
exile
opacity
precocious

#113
BOUQUET MUSE
Pick or buy yourself a couple of flowers or sprigs from a plant or tree to set upon your table and use as a muse in more than one way. Often, plants, especially aromatic barks and herbs, blooms and bulbs, can be captivating in fragrance as well as visual beauty. Texture adds another element. All combine to allow for experimentation with words...or, choose to use in your own way...

VOCABULARY WORDS:
cogent
dalliance
gilt
vagary

#114
INDEPENDENCE
Create a situation in which your character thinks he will be limited but he actually experiences independence and freedom. For example, maybe she thinks a new job will restrict her life, but it opens new possibilities that actually expand her worldview.
For nonfiction and poetry, apply it to yourself or someone you know.

VOCABULARY WORDS:
bashful
podium

resonance
sparkler

#115
CREATE A RECIPE
Grab a snack for yourself and create a scene in which your character creates a new recipe, even if they aren't a chef and your book has nothing to do with food. (Perhaps you won't even use this scene or the recipe, but use it as a writing exercise) Maybe the recipe flops or it could be a surprising success.
For nonfiction and poetry, apply it to yourself or someone you know.

VOCABULARY WORDS:
acerbic
avidity
deft
effervesce

#116
MORNING
Rise and shine! Does your character grab a power drink of fresh orange juice or a smoothie, and set herself up for success first thing in the morning? How does your character spend her mornings?
For nonfiction and poetry, apply it to yourself or someone you know.

VOCABULARY WORDS:
cumbersome
ennui
pastiche
streel

#117
TIME WASTE?
Create a situation in which your character is criticized for wasting time, but show that your character is actually accomplishing something and not simply daydreaming as a waste of time. Does your character inhabit another world when he daydreams? Where does he go and why is he escaping?

For nonfiction and poetry, explore the idea of daydreaming and imaginative time in your own life. Have you been criticized or even punished for your imaginative side? Have you stopped yourself from fulfilling and/or pursuing the ideas in your daydreams?

VOCABULARY WORDS:
augmentation
bolline
horary
kiln

#118
YOUR WRITING SPACE
Consider changing your actual writing space. Light a few candles and create a new atmosphere for your writing session. If candlelight writing isn't the type of new mood that would inspire you, find any new atmosphere for your writing. Have you ever written about your writing space or writing spaces that inspire you? Do these places show up your creative work?

WORDS:
errant
fulminate
risible
tallow

#119
GO OUTSIDE
Writers, get outside and write! Look around at your outdoor environment and try blending some elements into your writing. If getting outside isn't possible for you, imagine a scene in nature, describe the landscape by sight, smell, touch, sound, and taste.

If you can't get outside but you have access to the internet, look up a live webcam and watch the outside scene. Use it as inspiration to write.

WORDS:
amorphous
ingather
lull
ruminate

#120
LUCKY TALISMAN

Try using a lucky talisman as inspiration. Consider giving your character a lucky charm or superstition related to an object that she values.

For nonfiction and poetry, do you have a lucky talisman that helps you? How did you get it? Why do you think it's special? Write out one of the stories surrounding it.

WORDS:
agglomerate
epicure
fop
tapering

#121
TWO CHARACTERS MEET

Make forces collide for this writing prompt. Blend the lives of your characters. Write a scene in which characters from different stories meet. Or, try creating two or three new character sketches and then allow them to meet and see what new plot twists you can create for your writing, or maybe the characters will prompt a new style from you.

For nonfiction and poetry, create a situation in which people from different times in your life meet one another. These are people who don't know one another. Use your imagination to bring their dialogue to life.

WORDS:
concoction
malaise

spangle
welt

#122
FAVORITES
I asked some of my favorite people to tell me some of their favorite words, and I've included those words in a few prompts of The Nudge. You try it, too: Involve someone in your writing process. Ask them about a favorite place, person, or word, and use their perspective to inform your work's setting, characters, and/or phrases. Let them know why you're asking.
If you don't have someone to ask, look on social media platforms where people are constantly telling you about their favorite books, brands, places, people, and more. Pick one and go with it.
Don't forget to incorporate these words into your writing...this prompt's words were provided or inspired by my youngest daughter.

WORDS:
caper
elegant
lissome
love

#123
VISITOR'S EYES
Try your hand at travel-writing. Even if you aren't traveling, look around your surroundings and see with the eyes of a visitor or the eyes of a child. Change your point of view by sitting down to take photos or moving to a higher vantage point. Take a new road or route that isn't in your usual routine. Use this perspective to inform your writing and use a new angle in your story. Here are some words to throw in the mix. These words were either provided or inspired by Jennifer, a friend.

WORDS:
blithe
laud
mellifluous
thistle

#124
COLOR BLOCK
Focus on color *and* physical form in your writing. Show how the two work together to complement one another or how they contrast. Consider looking at artwork and fashion to help you with inspiration. You might choose to emphasize color and form through minimalism or boldly show color as overcoming form in your work. Use color and form as a focal point in your descriptions of setting. The absence color and form can also have a strong effect. Add these words which were either provided or inspired by my oldest daughter...

WORDS:
blister
comic
luminary
mandala

#125
DICTIONARY
Get out your toolboxes and find a good dictionary. In fact, try to use a dictionary in print form and not simply one on the internet. If you don't own a dictionary in print, visit your local public library and use theirs or buy one from a bookstore for your home. Add a dictionary to a scene in your story or poem.

WORDS:
adulatory
augury
corroboration
pendency

#126
THE SOUND OF WORDS
Are there words that you like to use simply because you enjoy the way that they sound? Do you shy away from speaking some words also due to their sounds? Try using these words that my husband

chose based on how pleasing and unique the words sound to us, and/or play around with some words that you don't use very often but that sound interesting to you.

WORDS:
brine
cardamom
ponder
sheathe

#127
FAD PHRASES

Consider words that you associate with a particular time, place, and/or person in your life or your character's life if you are writing fiction. Give some repetitive and particular words to a minor character in a story, or perhaps your minor character uses a word/phrase in a way that is unique, or you might consider giving your character a particular way of using a word during a specific period in her life, or maybe she uses a word or phrase for a short time and then abandons it like a fad or a group of friends that lasts only for a season, even if they are influential. Here are some words to try on for size...

WORDS:
mezzanine
sycophant
trundle
typify

#128
AWKWARD

Let's look at some awkward but intriguing words. Try working these words into your stories. Do you intentionally draw attention to the awkwardness of the word, or do you find some unique way of making the word fit in? Will attaching these words to a character or place create a fitting partnership and thereby a way to introduce words with which readers might have an aversion or be unfamiliar?

WORDS:
idiosyncrasy
pulchritude
shirr
star anise (Illicium verum)

#129
RHYTHM AND BEATS

Writers, we're making some noise for The Nudge! Find a rhythm in your work. Listen to the sounds of the words and create beats with movement in the work based on how the words sound and work together in meaning. Consider listening to Yusef Komunyakaa recite his poetry and/or the Beat poets and/or reading their work. Be punctilious in the process of playing with word acrobatics and sound compositions. Try these words out...

WORDS:
composure
mercy
punctilious
sherbet

#130
CHARACTER'S SIDE STORY

Create a scene in which your main character tells a story to a minor character. This could be a story about herself or off topic from personal revelation altogether, but use the storytelling moment to reveal your primary character's ability (or inability) to tell a story to someone else.

How do they tell a story? What does she give away to the listener too quickly, or does she go on and on until the listener is so bored that he realizes there is no point to the story, etc.? Does your main character exaggerate? Is he too modest when talking about his personal past and accomplishments? Does he tell stories to strangers that he meets, say, on an airplane or in an uber? Remember, interestingly, in this scene, you are now telling two or more stories by creating this type of situation in your overall story. For an added bonus, try to fit these words into the story...

WORDS:
canard
commendatory
perspicuous
raillery

#131
A SUMMER STORY I

Start writing a summer story. Be imaginative and inventive in pairing elements together for the summer. This season, maybe like no other, is possibly full of spontaneity, languorous days, adventure, and mystical nights. Read some stories that feature summer as inspiration: E.B. White's "Once More to the Lake" and Eudora Welty's "Why I Live at the P.O." Some words to throw in the mix...

WORDS:
hegemony
obduracy
sibilant
zinnia

#132
SUMMER STORY II— HEARTBREAKER

We've got a double header in this summer series. To continue the summer story for this prompt, you must step up to the plate and break your character's heart. Yes, heartbreaker. Quickly and swiftly, hit that scene out of the park.

Then, maybe a few scenes later, you allow him to have the ultimate moment of redemptive summer magic. Combine many elements in order to create a scene that blends several layers of the character's life. Perhaps, this is a moment when, as her heart mends, she realizes all the gratitude she has failed to give, but can to those who have been there all along. Or, maybe she finds her summer mojo and the mystical awareness of nature's presence within everyone. Perhaps, he falls in love again, but this time, he's smarter about how he gives his love away. Either way, give your character a scene of summer magic that changes his life. Throw these words in for an added challenge...

WORDS:
edict
razz
redolent
succor

#133
SUMMER STORY III— JUICY
Drift in some descriptive overplay. You can prune it back soon enough. Editing is on the horizon, but for this prompt, choose a scene or the whole story and describe everything fully, without holding back. If you use the summer story from the past two prompts, for example, then notice everything about the summer season as you write. Make the season come to life by saturating those scenes, making them juicy with descriptions. Here are some words to throw into the process...

WORDS:
bezel
luxuriant
nuance
whirl

#134
SUMMER STORY IV— POINT OF VIEW CHANGE
Change your narrative perspective for this prompt. Use the summer story and/or scene that you've been working on for the past couple of prompts. Choose a different character in the story and write the exact same scene or story from that other character's point of view. The character could be a minor character or an inanimate object, a plant, animal, or insect. The point is to change the perspective so that you are not focused on your main character's point of view. You might not like this exercise or keep the new version of the story created by this practice, but it is a great tool to sharpen your skills. It could also allow you to see your main character from another perspective. An added challenge would be to incorporate the following words...

WORDS:
blustery

callow
educe
riley

#135
UNFAMILIAR

Get out of your normal routine and explore. Go to a new park, restaurant, neighborhood, or some other location in your home town. Maybe you are on a vacation or a trip, if so, describe that place. Go beyond basic descriptions by comparing and contrasting the new place with somewhere you've spent a lot of time (maybe your home town as an adult or where you grew up in childhood), look for a range of characters by watching the people in the new location (locals and visitors or tourists), and consider how it feels to travel versus the comfort and/or boredom of being in a familiar place.

Another approach would be to look at what is valuable to the people and/or place where you are visiting versus what is valuable to the people/place where you usually reside.

WORDS:
fortune
impecunious
mellow
staidly

#136
STORM SCENE

Take a look back at your writing and add a storm scene to your story/poem. Does the storm build up over a long period of time, adding pressure and stress to the lives of the characters and/or the landscape? Perhaps the storm arrives suddenly out of nowhere, thundering into the scene. Is the storm a relief in some way? What type of storm, how long does it last, what changes in the process...these are some of the questions to answer in your writing. Check out Kate Chopin's short story "The Storm" for inspiration.

WORDS:
clabber

pliant
rend
tattler

#137
OPENING HOOK

Work on an opening scene. Revisit how your story opens and craft the first line so that it hooks the reader. Make that first line sound sharp and inviting. Set up the first scene to not only intrigue the reader with visual imagery, but lure them farther into the narrative with fragrance and taste. Often, scenes that involve enticement are openers that contain many delights for the reader and keep them wanting more. Words to mix in...

WORDS:
pluck
rufous
soothe
vice

#138
DRINK-INFUSED STORY

Try writing a drinking scene. This scene could revolve around the act of drinking alcohol, a place where alcohol is the main beverage of consumption, and/or the alcoholic beverage itself (how it is made, stored, etc.). Think beyond the typical alcoholic drinks that are portrayed in stories and movies. Furthermore, strive to show some depth of character beyond the character's relationship to drinking/a drink. Words to mix in...

WORDS:
deleterious
prosy
salutary
vintner

#139
RESEARCH PLANT SUPERSTITIONS

Consider the history of the tulip as you follow the writing nudge. The tulip bulb acquired a value more than gold in the world market back in the 1600s in Holland, where tulip mania had some devastating effects for a few. Use this as an example to do research about a particular flower. Learn about the habits and processses of the flower and note any interesting history and/or superstitions associated with the flower within human culture. Try to use those ideas, practices, and/or histories within your writing. Some words to sprinkle through the writing...

WORDS:
bless
expiate
germane
umbrage

#140
CHARACTER FLAWS

Choose some imperfections for your character. Perhaps these are only perceived imperfections that often work to the character's advantage, and/or focus on how your character comes to terms with or gains an understanding for her "flaws." Often, we make our characters perfect or ideal versions of people. Try making your characters show their humanity by pointing out their weaknesses or character flaws, and maybe you can turn those weaknesses into assets later in the story. Words to incorporate...

WORDS:
blemish
couchant
dirigible
sartorial

#141
STEREOTYPES

How common are stereotypes in your writing? Look at your work with a critical eye and be honest about how often you resort to stereotypes and clichés in order to transition and/or because you lacked the creativity at the time. Revisit those places and work on transforming the stereotypes or eliminating them altogether. Is there a time when a stereotype in your writing is useful or helpful?

WORDS:
flick
gondola
stymie
tisane

#142
MACHINERY

We're writing about machinery and/or patterns and routines that are completed with the use of machinery. Can you allow your writing to imitate machinery in some way? Consider sound, rhythm, control, precision, etc. We have some words to try with this process...

WORDS:
negligent
obsequious
prone
rancor

#143
FREEWRITE about PUDDLES

Allow the words to flow, pile, and puddle up. We're free-writing with wild abandon. Letting go is essential to getting a large number of words onto the page. It can also take you places in the narrative that you would never dared to explore without letting down your control devices. This is not a time to judge the words and story lines that emerge. Keep writing and don't look back! A few words to use...

WORDS:
luscious
perspicacious
reliquary
supine

#144
THAT OLD WORD

Practice using archaic words and use of language and dialogue from an historical era. Consider the idea of time travel, a dream sequence, or some type of similar scene that makes it easy to create the character and/or use the language differences between the present time period and the archaic language you are using in the story.

WORDS:
gambol
limn
puissant
transept

#145
ENDINGS

Start working on your endings. Some examples are the full circle ending, the cliffhanger, or an open-ended final page. What type of ending do you prefer as a reader? Do you enjoy stories that give you an uplifting tone at the end of the book, or are you more intrigued by a tragic or mysterious ending?

WORDS:
errant
lodestone
turnip
venerate

#146
LANDSCAPE

Focus on the landscape. If your story allows it, contrast the character's present landscape with one from their past, or maybe you show how the same landscape has been altered over time. Consider not only natural occurrences like plant and tree growth, but also how people and animals might have altered a landscape.

WORDS:
earthworks

endowment
temper
trust

#147
A BRIEF AFFAIR

We're writing a "get it while you can" scene. Craft a situation in which the character knows that they are getting something that won't last in the long run. This could be a physical thing, or it could be spending time in a certain a place. It might even be time with a person that creates a specific state of mind for the character. In the end, the character KNOWS that this is limited— whatever it is.

WORDS:
gallimaufry
mortar and pestle
numismatics
redound

#148
KNOW IT ALL

Create a "know it all" character. What are the specific topics about which he insists on giving his expertise? Is the character this way with everyone, or does she assert her insistence during particular situations? Does this way of being work out for him in the long run? You could use this character to add comic relief and/or aggravation. This character type is one way to share information with the reader.

WORDS:
effigy
furtive
heritable
transience

#149
ALL NIGHTER

Keep your character up all night. Write a scene or chapter in which your character is awake all night for some reason. She could be celebrating or she could be in a tortuous situation that annoys her and tests her patience. Either way, make your character pull an all-nighter.

WORDS:
ebullient
galley
paragon
sagacious

#150
INJURY
Give an injury to your main character or someone they know. The injury needs to deeply affect the character's life, whether it is her injury or not. Go beyond the physical injury and show how the injury changes the character's mental, emotional, social, and/or spiritual state of being. Even a minor injury has the potential to disrupt your character's routine.

As always, WORDS:
billow
dabble
middling
parry

#151
TOPSY TURVY PARTY
Your characters are getting dressed up for "The Freaker's Ball." Send them into a Halloween party, or otherwise, topsy-turvy party for the evening. This could be a very brief moment in your overall story, or it could be the entire setting.
Writers, make yourself a power shot of OJ, a cocktail of colorful and questionable contents, crack your knuckles, and write a dressed-up party scene to remember.

WORDS:
finalize
heirloom
lurid

macaroon

#152
MONSTER REVISITED

Writers, we're creating monsters and mythological creatures, a practice as old as the human mind. Use a monster of old and place her in the modern world and/or create a new story for him. Consider the novel *Grendel* by John Gardner who gives a voice to a medieval monster or Anne Rice's *Vampire Chronicles.* These monsters that you use in your writing could be unique such as the Cyclops or a group like the sirens. Either way, create your own monster character from a monster or mythological creature based in antiquity.

WORDS:
courteous
discern
gibe
lenitive

#153
CHILD'S SUPERHERO

Try writing a superhero or other character from a child's point of view. Show your superhero as a child. You might also want to continue developing your monster, and if so, show your monster when she was a youth in some way.

WORDS:
benefic
despotic
salient
triumphant

#154
MONSTER DEVELOPMENT

Continue with developing your monster or villain. The best ones have a likable quality, whether that is an attribute that raises them up OR one that brings them down to earth (that depends on your monster), create a quality that likens the monster and/or villain to the reader, to a human. If the monster is lofty and snobby, you might show a way that she chooses to be average. If the villain is gritty and full of muck, you might show his intelligence and/or kindness.

WORDS:
bauble
effete
nonplus
sardonic

#155
AUTUMN

Look around, and take a walk in your mind if the season is not autumn where you live right now. Consider a particularly autumn fragrance and write about that. You could also try writing about the flavors that are specific to autumn. Take a stroll through an autumn garden and try the herbs, maybe even the familiar ones, and see if they are different now. Fall fruits, nuts, and berries are another way to explore this season in your writing.

WORDS:
abjure
cogitate
ruby
votary

#156
WEAKNESS

Let's focus on symbolism. Create a symbol of weakness for your character. This is something that debilitates her and drains her of power and strength. The weakness doesn't have to be as dramatic as comic book characters, but it's the same idea. The weakness could be temporary, as if a storm rolled through your character's life (maybe she didn't see this weakness coming), but it might also be the type of storm that makes a big impact (think, tornado-type of damage resulting from the character giving in to the weakness). Big impact or minor role, we all have our weaknesses, so make sure to give one to your character.

WORDS:
abscess
bereft
erudite
tawdry

#157
SPIRITUAL POWER

Create a spiritual object of enchantment in your story— this is something that has special power(s) whether by magical property, spiritual endowment, and/or the characters' belief. The object might not be special at all, but only seems so by the character's belief that it is, or you might add that element to your story (Excalibur, the sword of King Arthur, in Arthurian Legend is an example of an object of enchantment and/or one believed to be so and questioned at the same time).

WORDS:
congenial
locket
tryst
will o' the wisp

#158
SWIMMING

Allow your character to go swimming. This swimming scene could be anywhere— scuba diving into the depths of the sea, a hot lagoon in Iceland, a swimming pool at his girlfriend's parents' beach house, a big old-fashioned bathtub, a muddy pond, her daughter's kiddie pool in the backyard, at the end of the dock on the lake...wherever it is, fully describe your character's experience.

WORDS:
bellow
pacify
truculent
twilight

#159
POLITICS
Write a scene in which your character is affected by politics or a political decision. Consider a political decision made about the environment that affects the area where she lives or visit, and/or maybe a new law is enacted that changes how his parents are able to conduct their business. These are just two example scenarios.

WORDS:
cordial
foreword
mawkish
paralyzed

#160
SHOPPING
Take your character out shopping somewhere, and allow him to be in an observant mood. Perhaps this is an exceptionally rare time of exchange, and she witnesses something special in a store. Or, maybe you allow your character to notice his estrangement from a particular side of the economic culture (this could be his home culture or one he is visiting). Either way, this scene should show choices and learning from the experience of purchasing.

WORDS:
bushy
dredge
saga
twist

#161
BIRDS
Add the symbol of a bird or a bird to your story or poem. Birds have the ability to fly, even into foreboding or otherwise impenetrable situations. Learn about the birds that inhabit the setting of your book. If you are writing science fiction with new landscape, consider creating your own birds for the story.

WORDS:

dazzling
dulcet
calumniate
savant

#162
HOLIDAY BEGINNING
Write a fresh start for your character that happens around a holiday celebration. A new beginning for your characters! This could be any holiday, really, but consider the winter holidays of Diwali, Hanukah, Winter Solstice, Yule, Christmas and/or New Years. For inspiration: In books, the all-time favorite, *A Christmas Carol.* Perhaps the ending is the place where the reader discovers that the character's life will change.

WORDS:
assail
betoken
nourish
shandy

Historically-Based Prompts
163 - 180

The Nudge is going back in time. Get ready to dabble in some other time and place, or dig in and research the finer details of an era. Maybe you write poems inspired by these prompts, or spend time on a longer work of historical fiction that weaves in and out of human history, or perhaps something in between is on your itinerary. Above all, have fun in this time machine— you never know where we'll go and what I'll choose to explore.

#163
Europe, 17th century, Changing Seasons Celebration

Let's make the first prompt broad and somewhat easy to find a lot of information in your research. Learn about any culture and location in 17th century Europe where the changing of the seasons was celebrated in some way. Try writing a fictional story set in that time period, or compose a poem that contrasts or compares a modern celebration with one from that time period.

One example is Carnival, believed to have been originally celebrated to honor the rebirth of the Earth (Spring), though the debates continue on the origins of Carnival, which make it and other historically-based celebrations intriguing settings for your creative work.

#164
Time Travel: South America, 19th century, Travel Accommodations

For this historical writing prompt, we're staying with any time during a full century— the 19th century this time— and a large, general location— anywhere in South America— and any type of travel and/or accommodations as our thematic focus. You might approach this by doing some research on what it might have been like to make a journey to Brazil in 1877, for example, or perhaps you choose how one village in Peru might deliver communications and/or trade goods with another during 1834.

Find an article to read, a documentary to watch, a book from an online library to aid you in your research endeavors.
As always, choose to write in your own style— poetry, nonfiction, journaling, a fictional short story, part of a historically-inspired novel, or a mixture of genres and styles.

#165
Time Travel: Patterns of Sleep during antiquity. Any place.

It's time to delve into patterns of sleep and how they have changed over time. Think about how humans have slept in shifts for various reasons throughout history, and how the luxury of eight hours or more of uninterrupted and, otherwise, "safe" sleep is a modern development. You might compare a time in the past to situations in our current time when people are still sleeping in shifts, due to necessity.

For example, other reasons that people have slept in shifts or stages have included tending a fire, tending a kitchen stove, patrolling and watching for intruders and invaders, watching for signals, watching for animals, looking out for livestock, looking out for crops, waiting for transportation, and so on and so forth.

Or, maybe you approach this differently, and research some stories about sleep and dreams. How have opinions about dreams and what they mean changed over time?

#166
Time Travel: The Americas, 1800s, Plant Lore & Herbal Remedies

Do some research on plant lore during the 1800s, anywhere in North or South America. You might consider superstitions about plants or indigenous herbal remedies. Show how your character might use both wild and tame plants.

For poetry, focus on heirloom plants— write a poem from the perspective of one heirloom plant.
If journaling, look at any of your family remedies that could have been passed down through the generations. What are they? Do they connect to a particular time or place?

You could also approach this by reflecting changes in plant usage and consumption— growing, harvesting, processing, and distributing plants— for decoration, for products, for food, for medicine...and so much more.

Examples: In *Poke Sallet Queen & the Family Medicine Wheel*, I write about the rituals and celebrations, as well as the recipes and practical use of poke sallet, or pokeweed. In *Ripe for the Pickin',* I continue this focus on plants and plant lore and write about a variety of plants.

#167
Time Travel: Jewelry, Family Heirloom, Any Place, Any Time

Go to any time and place, but allow jewelry to transport you there. Jewelry is often endowed with magical properties, for good or ill, or some combination in between. It can also offer a mystery component. For this Nudge, write a historical flashback scene or a poem or essay based on a piece of jewelry that is a family heirloom or an antique.

Some inspiration: The mythological "ancient" world and quest for the ring in *The Lord of the Rings* Trilogy by J.R.R. Tolkien; and the necklace in the poem "Unending Love" by Rabindranath Tagore and many more examples in poetry.
In *Poke Sallet Queen & the Family Medicine Wheel*, I write about a ring from a jewelry store that was historically famous in Nashville, TN, where my novel is set.

#168
Time Travel: Pictures from the Archives Where You Currently Live

Time travel in the town where you live. If possible, visit your local archives or museum, in person or on line, and use a historical photo of the place where you currently live as a writing prompt. First, free-write about the photo before you know a lot of details about that time in history and why it may be significant. Step into the photograph and tell a story. Maybe add some research to your story, learn about it, change, and add to the story over time.

In my novel, *Ripe for the Pickin',* I used a photograph of an unknown Fisk University graduate from the 19th century and allowed my character to describe the same photograph as a character in the book.

#169
Time Travel: 1920s, Any place, An Advertisement for a toiletry item or personal care product

Use an advertisement from the 1920s, anywhere in the world, to write based on that toiletry or personal care product or advertisement. Perhaps you'll learn about product in the past that is no longer in use or was deemed harmless, perhaps even healthy and beneficial, when it was introduced but was discovered to be harmful, even deadly, later. You might also use advertisements from the 1920s to learn about slang terms or phrases that are no longer in use or have changed in meaning since that time.

#170
Time Travel: 19th century, Any place, A Game

Research a game that was played during the 19th century and work this game into your story. Maybe this is a game that originated in the 19th century but is still played today, or perhaps it's a game that most people are no longer familiar with. This could be a card game or something similar or it might be an athletic game. Consider all the different styles of games that people can play, and what competition and sport mean in cultures around the world.

#171
Time Travel: 1970s, Music, Any place

Alright, this should be an easy one. Play a record or an 8-track if you've got one, but find some 1970s tunes to inspire you while you write. Remember that you can't quote from a song without permission, but you can reference musicians and songs in your writing. You can certainly set the mood for your characters.

#172
Time Travel: 19th century, Disease, Any place

Look up diseases from the 19th century. You might choose one that is still hanging around and compare its past to how deadly and/or prevalent it is during contemporary times. You could also look at a disease that has changed in how it affects the human body.
Describe the social conditions that contributed to both the spread and the containment of the disease. Was a cure and/or vaccination discovered, created, and/or invented for the disease? Is there a treatment for the residual effects if there are any?

#173
Time Travel: 1960s, Fashion, Any place

Check out the range of fashion in the 1960s, from the beginning to the start of the 1970s. Show how the fashion changed. Use this as a chance to tell a story through the fads or through the music-inspired fashions and/or both.

#174
Time Travel: Any Time, Any place, The Creation of a Famous Artwork

NOT the Mona Lisa! Choose another famous work of art— painting, sculpture, drawing, architecture, etc.— and write a story about how that work of art was conceived and/or created. You might choose to write a fictional story about the artwork or the artist, or perhaps you do some research and write a nonfiction story or poem about it.

#175
Time Travel: Any place, Any Time, Photos of a Historical Person

Think about someone famous in history that you've always been curious about but who you've never really learned about. First, find some photos of that person, but don't read about them yet. Free-write about that person after looking at three different photos of them. Then, read and learn more about them.

How does your writing match up with information you learned about them later? If it doesn't, could you use this writing to develop a new character? Could you use this writing about the historical person? Are you more curious about them now?

#176
Time Travel: 18th century, Any place, A Battle

Learn about a battle from the 18th century and create a character who finds themselves in a heroic situation even though he or she had never been heroic before in life. Consider the climate in the battle. What is the weather like? The landscape? The cultural climate that led to battle?

#177
Time Travel: 1990s, Any place, A Famous Book

Check out the books from the 1990s and grab something that has fallen out of fashion now. Use this book to show a particular type of influence or style or both. You might consider carrying themes from that book throughout your own in a humorous or satirical way. Maybe your character is obsessed with the book and demands that someone in her life read it, or perhaps she rearranges her whole life based on something she read in the book. Does she forget about the book later? Does she remember the significance of it in her life?

Does she meet the author or reread the book again and again throughout her life?

#178
Time Travel: WWII, Music, Any place

Write a story about World War II using music so that it is more than background. Allow the music to guide your characters. Maybe a song, a band, a record plays a pivotal role in their lives. Maybe music helps them in ways that nothing else can. Is it an escape? Is it a promise that life still exists, that happiness and love are still present in the world? Does music betray them? Does music serve as their salvation?

#179
Time Travel: 1930s, Roles of Women and Men, Any Place

Explore the roles of women and men in the 1930s through a character who wants to live a life atypical of their gender. This could be how they dress, where they work, how they want to work, how they want to teach children about gender roles, how they view social roles and constraints, and how they push particular boundaries.

#180
Time Travel: 1890-1919, Any place, Dance Trends

Look at the dance trends at the turn of the 20th century. Did any of the dances or cultural views of dancing change significantly? What became fashionable and does it seem to be an advancement, a setback, a reaction, etc? How can you incorporate this into your story or show this in a poem?

Creative Writing Basics
Prompts 181 - 186

The Nudge is going back to the basics of creative writing. Whether you are a seasoned writer who has applied these techniques and tools to spring, summer, winter, fall, and every setting in between including some in other universes, or a beginner who doesn't really know how to even list creative writing basics, then it's time to play around and have some fun. Our definitions will be brief, but there are ample online sources to provide you with longer definitions and more examples.

#181
Back to Creative Writing Basics: Alliteration

We begin with **alliteration,** which is the repetition of sounds (usually consonants in the beginning syllable of a word) with two or more other words close by.

For example, from *Talking Underwater* by Melissa Corliss DeLorenzo, alliteration is the repetition of "r" in this sentence: "(...) The raspy sand rubs..."And even from the review by Sheri Holman for *Talking Underwater,* Holman uses alliteration a few times: "By turns tender and tragic, this is the most generous and genuine story of sisterly love I've read in ages."

#182
Back to Creative Writing Basics: Personification

Personification: giving human qualities to something inhuman and/or inanimate. For example, "I like pink. It's as if red is whispering to me."— S. Teague from *Seasons of Balance: On*

Creativity and Mindfulness. In the example, S. Teague writes as if the color red is a person who can whisper.

Choose an inanimate object to "bring to life" in a piece of your writing. Or, like S. Teague, maybe pick a color to personify in your writing.

#183 - 184
Back to Creative Writing Basics: Simile and Metaphor

The Nudge is going back to the basics of creative writing. As always, our definitions will be brief, but there are ample online sources to provide you with longer definitions and more examples.

Simile: comparing two or more things using the words "like" or "as" in the phrase.

Metaphor: comparison of two or more things, and the comparison can be a direct or indirect reference.

For example, "She felt the vibration on her sides and imagined **OM birds fluttering back and forth inside of her body--inside the cages of her bones.** (...) Mia closed her eyes. She began to vibrate with the OM sound, lightly and quietly at first. She heard the yogis from her dad's class join in softly and **they hummed like little honeybees** combing the fields of clover. **Their fuzzy heads were like the bees' fuzzy legs.** She...."
From my book, *The Adventures to Pawnassus.*

First, you can see the metaphor of the birds being lungs, the ribs being a cage containing birds. Second, there are two similes using the word "like". You could substitute "as" instead of "like" there, for example: "...they hummed as little honeybees..."

Set up a scene in your writing and add another layer with similes and metaphors.

#185
Back to Creative Writing Basics: Onomatopoeia

The Nudge is going back to the basics of creative writing. As always, our definitions will be brief, but there are ample online sources to provide you with longer definitions and more examples.

Onomatopoeia: a word that imitates a sound. Some examples: "...it **slithered** around her..." "...taunting and ready to **strike**" "...from the **spark** that lit..." "...**swarmed** within..." These examples are from *A Momentary Darkness* by Nikki Martin. She also combines onomatopoeia with alliteration in the following phrase: "It was a wave washing..."
Some common examples of onomatopoeia are sounds that imitate animals: cuckoo, woof, meow, moo.

Other common onomatopoeias: sizzle, hiss, bang, poof, etc.
Have some fun and play around with imitating the sounds around your characters. Action stories like *A Momentary Darkness* provide many opportunities to accentuate sound, but so do poetry and essays when you need and want to emphasize a particular sound.

#186
Back to Creative Writing Basics: Stream of Consciousness

Stream of Consciousness: Stream of consciousness is a style of writing and a creative writing technique. The writer decides to write whatever comes into the mind in a continuous flow or stream, writing the thought patterns as they emerge and recede from the mind, and oftentimes, circle back around again in theme or with the use of full phrases.
A famous example is the poem, "The Love Song of J. Alfred Prufrock" by T.S. Eliot.

Revision
Prompts 187 - 190

#187

Toolbox: REVISION using ACTION VERBS

Find a scene in your story that needs speed/momentum in the tone. This scene might not contain action in the typical way. The momentum could only be in the mind of your character. Choose verbs that will propel the scene forward, even if only in the character's mind (for example, fear and anxiety-laden moments where no real action occurs). Practice using strong action verbs.

Additional advice for nonfiction prose and poetry: Focus on time in your life when you created more momentum and action in your mind and then realized that the events didn't measure up to the scenario in your head. Write a poem using words that invoke action and/or momentum. Consider how words sound when choosing them.

#188

Tool: REVISION of a flashback scene with emphasis on REVERIE/NOSTALGIA/REGRET

Writers, reach in your toolbox and get out your eraser. We're working on revision. Peruse your story and find a scene in which you use a flashback within another larger story. You'll work on revising the flashback scene with a greater depth in mind. You could do this by adding a moment of extended dialogue or a thought pattern, an awareness, of reverie and/or regret. This moment could be nostalgic or remorseful, or both. Give your character some awareness about the passage of time. You could elevate the flashback scene so that it no longer remains on the sidelines as a side story, but becomes a deeper reflection of time. Consider making your main emphasis about the concept and process of aging in a thoughtful and profound scene for your character.

Additional advice for creative nonfiction and poetry: Peruse your writings and find a poem, essay, or creative nonfiction story with some thematic focus on time and/or aging. Consider revising it with more awareness on highlighting the passage of time. Polish a poem that emphasizes time-awareness so that it reaches out toward the reader as well, going beyond the personal experience of aging and timing, and invoking and enveloping the reader into that experience of time moving forward and/or backward. Play around with ways to do that by both directly involving and speaking to the reader, even using the reader in experimental ways, and indirectly triggering the reader's consciousness of time in some way. Revise, experiment, and have fun!

#189
Tool: READ with minor revisions
Writers, it can't be all character creation and fun descriptions of fake worlds. Yes, it's still all of that, but you're making your writing much better for everyone outside of your head if you revise the manuscript and do a read-through of your own work. It's your responsibility to revise your own work, first. Expecting others to do the dirty work for you in every way causes the work to suffer by your inability to use the depth of talent available from editors. Edit the main things and leave the rest to the editors.

If you see a mistake, fix it! Don't wait for an editor. The editors can then give you more advanced editing suggestions instead of being mired in your typos. Enjoy the reading, and hopefully you will find both your strengths and weaknesses as a writer.

One of the most helpful ways you can "see" your manuscript is by reading it aloud, whether that is only to yourself or to a friend, family member, or colleague. Just be sure that if you include someone else in this reading, that you note their recommendations after you finish the story. Ask them to keep notes about their opinions, and not to share their thoughts with you until the manuscript reading is complete. Be selective about including someone else, as some influences could suggest alterations that could harm the work and you as a writer.

#190

Tool: DIRTY WORK, Manuscript Checklist

Now, it's time to do the dirty work if you haven't already. Ensure that the manuscript is all typed in the same font, preferably a font that is easy to read for a variety of readers (Times New Roman, Helvetica, and Georgia are a few examples). Complete a spelling and grammar check. Make sure all the big issues are correct: Section and chapter breaks, paragraph breaks, and title changes to chapters and sections. For the sake of consistency, complete a "Find/Replace" for character name changes that you made. Finally, make sure that your manuscript has a main title.

Use the following blank space to make a list of the manuscript revisions that you need to complete:

Self-Reflection
Prompts 191 – 203

Free-write your answers to the following topics and questions about yourself as a writer and how you view your own writing and writing goals.

#191
FATALISM
Question: How has your view of your own story messed you up or controlled your writing career?

#192
SELF-AWARENESS
Question: How do you see yourself as a writer now?

#193
BACKGROUND
Question: What are some of your writing achievements? If you are a great blogger or social media writer who has gained a significant following, then use that to describe your writing strengths. Have you written short articles or business pieces? Do you excel at giving speeches and presentations? Write out all of your writing strengths.

#194
IMAGINE
Question: What do you want to achieve as a writer? Give in to all of your daydreams and big ideas and write them down, even the things that seem impossible.

#195

FAMILIAR

Question: Who are some writers that you have emulated or whose style is similar to yours?

#196

EVENT

Question: Name one writer event that you can do soon or that you can sign up to do. Do a little research if you aren't aware of one. Is there an open mic night where you can read aloud? Maybe there's a writing group that you could join, or a class that you could take? Find a writing event and go for it.

#197

SYNOPSIS

Question: Try your hand at writing a synopsis of your story, book, and/or collection of poetry. Start out by crafting three to four sentences about it, and try to get two paragraphs for a longer work. Then ask someone to read and/or listen to your synopsis. Did they get it? Do they understand what your story is about, in a basic way?

#198

READER/EDITOR

Question: Ready to give your book to a reader/editor for honest feedback?

#199

ONE STEP

Question: Name one step that you can take toward achieving a big writing goal.

#200

SUBMISSIONS

Question: Have you submitted your story, book, and/poem for publication yet? Choose one publication/publisher/agent that you think would be a good fit for your story, poem, or book and look up the submission process.

#201
PROMOTION/SELF CONFIDENCE
Question: Have you created a marketing page for yourself either on a website or social media platform or both? Are you confident about talking about yourself as a writer, as someone seeking publication, as someone with a book to share? How can you begin telling people about yourself as a writer, your story, your journey, and all of the above?

#202
ON TRACK
Question: What can you do to keep yourself on track right now?

Do you need to write every day in order to finish a book? Set a routine and stick with it, knowing that each day you are closer to reaching the goal of a complete book.

Do you need to make a new list of outlets for your writings? Then, do a little research and find publications that will fit your new work?

Do you need inspiration? Go back through these writing prompts and find new sources of imagination and wonder.

Do you need a coach? Place a list of affirmations around your house and your writing spaces in order to coach you regularly to be confident in your writing.

Revisit the idea of being on track again and again since the list of goals for a writer and a writing project are always changing.

#203
NEW FORM
Question: Can you turn a past book into something new— a screenplay, a stage play, a series? Revisit a piece of writing from your past and put it into a new form. If you don't know how to write a screenplay, sign up for a class. Allow yourself to try new forms of writing so that you are always learning and refining your craft.

Acknowledgements

Thank you to everyone who has read these writing prompts online over the years.

Thank you, Terry, for encouraging another book.

About the Author

SHANA THORNTON is the author of three novels, *Ripe for the Pickin'* (2022), *Poke Sallet Queen and the Family Medicine Wheel* (2015), and *Multiple Exposure* (2012), and the young adult book, *The Adventures to Pawnassus* (2019). She is the author of *The Nudge: Writing Prompts* (2023) and co-author of the nonfiction self-help book, *Seasons of Balance: On Creativity and Mindfulness* (2016). Shana is a series editor for the BreatheYourOMBalance[R] book series. She is the Founder of the Clarksville Montgomery County African American Legacy Trail (2019).

For information about authors, books, upcoming reading events, new titles, and more, visit thorncraftpublishing.com